Candlesticks & Chart Trading Mastery

A Comprehensive Guide to Make Money Trading Candlesticks and Chart Patterns

Kritesh Abhishek

notionpress.com

INDIA • SINGAPORE • MALAYSIA

ISBN 979-8-89322-699-7

CONTENTS

ABOUT THE AUTHOR

Kritesh Abhishek is a Stock Trader, Value investor, and an Indian Entrepreneur with over ten years of experience of trading and investing in the Share Market. He is the founder of Trade Brains and FinGrad, two popular stock market Startups in India.

Kritesh has an undergraduate degree in electrical engineering from the National Institute of Technology, Warangal (Class of 2016). He is popularly known for writing his investing and trading blogs about the stock market that are published on Tradebrains. in with millions of monthly readers.

After completing his graduate education at the NITW, Kritesh joined Tata Motors in Pune, Maharashtra, where he worked as a senior manager in the product quality department of commercial vehicles for about one and a half years. In 2017, he left the job and decided to pursue his trading and entrepreneurial aspirations in Bengaluru. At the age of 23, Kritesh incorporated his first company, Dailyraven Technologies Private Limited.

Initially, Trade Brains was established as a website to spread awareness about the stock market. However, the platform evolved to encompass additional verticals, including stock market analytics and market news. This expansion proved successful as Trade Brains went on to attract over one million visitors monthly. Under Kritesh's leadership, the Trade Brains team has grown from a solitary member to a thriving staff of over forty-five individuals. Additionally, the platform has built a strong social media presence, boasting over 800K followers across multiple platforms including Instagram and YouTube.

In 2022, Kritesh launched his second educational venture, FinGrad (Incorporated as Fingrad Ventures Private Limited), as a financial learning platform that provides a variety of stock market training, both online and offline. Its website has over 75,000 registered users and aims to be a comprehensive destination for all financial education needs, offering a diverse range of financial courses and classes, including Technical Analysis, Fundamental Analysis, Futures and Options Trading, Commodity Trading, and many other financial concepts.

Kritesh has been invited as a guest speaker at various institutions including Symbiosis Institute of Business Management (SIBM) in Pune, Vellore Institute of Technology (VIT) in Vellore, Tamil Nadu, National Institute of Technology in Warangal, Telangana, and others, where he shared his expertise in stock market trading.

ACKNOWLEDGMENT

I am profoundly grateful for the opportunity to write this book and extend my heartfelt thanks to all those who have played a role, both direct and indirect, in its creation.

First and foremost, I owe a debt of gratitude to Aaron Vas and Gurudarshan D for their invaluable contributions to this work. Their insights, expertise, and unwavering support have been instrumental in bringing this project to fruition. Their dedication to excellence and willingness to share their knowledge have enriched this book immeasurably.

To my parents, Mr. Analesh Nandan and Mrs. Suman Sinha, whose unwavering love, guidance, and encouragement have been the bedrock of my journey, I offer my deepest thanks. Your belief in me has been a constant source of inspiration, driving me to push the boundaries of my creativity and pursue my dreams with determination.

I am also indebted to my wife, Shivani Soni, whose unwavering support and understanding have sustained me through the challenges of writing this book. Her patience, encouragement, and belief in my abilities have been my guiding light, motivating me to persevere even when faced with obstacles.

Furthermore, I extend my sincere appreciation to my colleagues, friends, and fellow traders who have cheered me on every step of the way. Your encouragement, feedback, and unwavering belief in this endeavor have been invaluable. Whether through insightful discussions, words of encouragement, or simply lending an empathetic ear, your support has kept me motivated and inspired throughout the writing process.

In addition, I would like to express my gratitude to Hitesh Singhi and the entire Trade Brains team, whose expertise and assistance have contributed to the success of this book.

I offer my deepest thanks to all those mentioned and countless others who have touched my life in meaningful ways. Your support, encouragement, and belief in me have made this journey possible; I am eternally grateful for that.

With Gratitude,

Kritesh Abhishek

INTRODUCTION TO TECHNICAL ANALYSIS

There are two common approaches to analyse and make money in the stock market. The first approach is the fundamental analysis, which is commonly used by long-term investors to generate wealth. On the other hand, Technical Analysis, which is another common approach, is used by day traders and short-term traders to make regular profits from the market on a day-to-day basis.

Fundamental analysis and technical analysis follow a completely different route in terms of principles, strategies, methodology and more. Before we start our discussion on candlesticks and charts, we must understand what Technical Analysis is and the difference between Fundamental and Technical Analysis. Let's get started.

Fundamental vs Technical Analysis

Fundamental analysis checks how lucrative a company is for long-term investment by looking into fundamental qualities and comparing it to its competitors and industry. This approach involves the study of everything related to the company, like its financial statements, Financial Ratios, Management, Competitors, Business models, industry analysis, Economy analysis, Competitive Advantage analysis or Moat analysis, market valuation, etc. Fundamental analysis is a comprehensive and time-consuming analysis approach.

On the other hand, Technical analysis does not care about the financials or the fundamentals of the companies but rather evaluates the company based on price movements, Charts, Patterns, Volume, momentum and more. Technical analysts use current and historical price charts to predict and identify future trends and movements.

Technical analysis is used for short-term analysis of stocks to make profits in a shorter period. As the holding period while using this approach is very short (sometimes even within minutes), the technical analysis does not care about the company's long-term plans, which are always checked by the fundamental analysis.

Now that we have a little understanding of both fundamental and technical analysis of stocks, let us discuss both these analysis approaches in detail based on a few key criteria.

1. Basic Principle & Methodology

- **The Fundamental analysis** approach analyses all the factors that can affect the stock price of a company in the future like its current and predicted financials, management, industry, competitors, business etc. It evaluates the valuation of the company to find whether the stock is underpriced or overpriced to purchase.
- **Technical analysis** reads the price charts, patterns, and trends of the stocks to predict their future price movement. They believe that future price patterns resonate with past movements.

2. Time Frame

- **The fundamental analysis** approach is used for long-term investment purposes.

- **The technical analysis** approach is used for short-term investments and can be used for scalping, day trading, swing trading Or positional trading

3. Data Sources

- **Fundamental analysts** gather data for analysis from annual reports, financial statements, the company's websites and other key company announcements, along with other economic news sources.
- **Technical analysts** gather data from the historical stock price charts and other price-related data like volume, patterns and more.

4. Indicators

- **Fundamental analysis** studies financial statements and financial ratios like assets, liabilities, earnings, expenses, Price to Earnings ratio, PB ratio, Debt/Equity ratio, ROE, ROCE, etc.
- **Technical analysis** uses different charts like candlesticks, line chart, point and figure chart and studies various technical indicators for their analysis like MACD, Simple Moving Average, EMA, RSI, Bollinger Bands, etc.

5. Strategy

- **Fundamental analysis** is used to find a healthy company to invest for long term by looking into its financials and valuations in order to evaluate whether the stock is overpriced or underpriced for purchase and to forecast the growth potential of the company.
- **Technical analysis** is used to find the right entry and exit time from the stock by looking at the charts and patterns in order to make quick decisions and profits on a short-term basis.

Pros and Cons of Fundamental Analysis

Here are a few of the best advantages of fundamental analysis:

- Fundamental analysis helps to invest in financially and qualitatively healthy companies, which is always a good approach.
- It helps the investors to generate big returns in the long term.

Here are a few of the common disadvantages or cons of fundamental analysis:

- Fundamental analysis is quite laborious, and its methodology is lengthy & complex.
- There is no clear time frame for long-term investment.
- As the future potential of the company is considered in the fundamental analysis, various assumptions are made in this approach, such as future growth, current valuation, etc. The assumptions may turn out to be wrong in future.
- As the entry & exit times are not specified in the fundamental analysis, you might buy a good stock at a wrong time.
- Fundamental analysis, like any other analysis approach, doesn't guarantee good returns. You might hold a fundamentally healthy stock for years with zero or negative returns.

Pros and Cons of Technical Analysis

Now let us discuss a few of the top pros and cons of Technical Analysis. Here are a few of the best advantages of Technical Analysis:

- Technical analysis is fast, and the outcomes can be seen quite quickly. As the trades may last for minutes, hours or a few months, the results of whether you are profitable or in loss can be known early.
- This approach is comparatively less laborious.
- Entry and exit time for the stock can be specified and readily give buy or sell indications.

Nonetheless, no analysis is perfect. Here are a few of the common disadvantages of the technical analysis approach:

- As there are hundreds of technical indicators, it's tough to select the perfect indicator that works the best for you.
- Technical analysis skills require a lot of accuracy, reliability, and discipline.

Note: An important point to note is that fundamental analysis and technical analysis can also be used together. It makes sense to buy a fundamentally strong company at the right time. While fundamental analysis helps to find a healthy company to invest in, technical analysis tells you the right time to enter or exit that stock by looking into its charts.

In this book, we'll focus on the Technical Analysis aspects of trading in stocks and will majorly study candlestick patterns, the most popular charting tool in the trading community, along with covering other popular chart patterns and indicators.

WHAT ARE CANDLESTICKS?

Candlestick chart is the most popular type of charting tool used by traders all over the world. This pattern was first developed by a Japanese rice trader named 'Homma Munehisa', who traded in the Dōjima Rice Exchange in Osaka during the Tokugawa Shogunate in the early 1700s. The candlestick pattern was later popularised by Charles Dow in the 1900s and remains the widely used price chart today in the financial market.

A candlestick pattern will tell you the four important price points of a security or an asset in a specific time period, namely the opening price (O), the high (H), the low (L), and the closing price (C).

For example, let's say that a share was trading at Rs 100 at 10:00 AM on a trading day, and we want to make a candlestick pattern for the same share for a time period of 5 minutes, i.e. between 10:00 AM and 10:05 AM. During this time period, the price of the security will keep fluctuating. However, let's assume that, after opening at Rs 100, the share price first went downwards and made a low of Rs 80, then it started moving upwards and made a high of Rs 120 and finally closed at Rs 110 at 10:05 AM.

Here, the Opening Price (O) is Rs 100, the high (H) is Rs 120, the low (L) is Rs 80, and the closing price (C) is Rs 110.

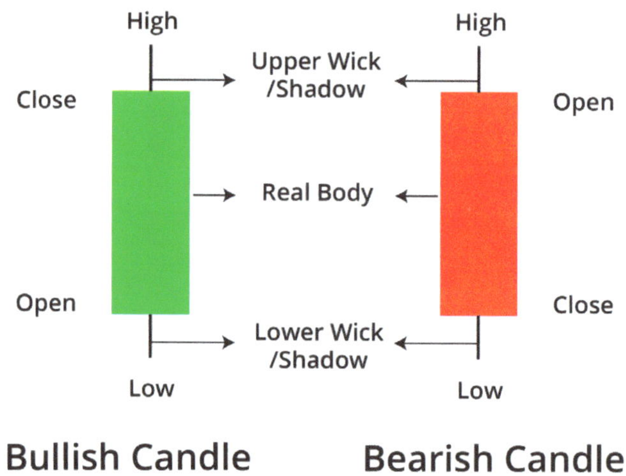

Fig. Basics of Candlestick Formation

A candlestick pattern comprises two parts, namely the body and the wick.

A. **Body:** The body of the candlestick indicates the opening and closing of the security. In other words, if you join the opening and closing of the candlestick pattern during the specified time period, you'll get its body.

B. **Wick:** The wick of the candlestick indicates the high and low of the security. It is attached to the body of the candle and can be of two parts, namely the upper wick and the lower wick, depending on its location compared to the body of the candle.

Now, a candle stick can be divided into two categories, namely the Bullish Candle and the bearish candle, depending on the opening and the closing of the candle during the time period.

A candlestick can be divided into two categories:

- **Bullish Candle:** A candle is said to be bullish when the closing price of the candle is greater than the opening price. It means that the prices of the security have gone up and closed at a higher price during this time period. This type of candle pattern is generally specified with a candle having a green (or white) body or simply green coloured candlestick pattern.
- **Bearish Candle:** A candle is said to be bearish when its closing price is lower than the opening price in the specified time period. It means that the prices of the security have gone down during this time period and closed at a lower price. Generally, this type of candle pattern is specified with a candle having a red (or black) body or simply red coloured candlestick pattern.

Types of Candlestick Patterns

Now, let us also look at the types of candlestick patterns based on the number of candles in consideration.

1. Single Candlestick Pattern

Single candle patterns are those patterns that are formed by just a single candle. If found right, here, the single candle patterns can help you judge whether the trade is going to be bullish, bearing or neutral.

A few of the popular single candlestick patterns are Bullish Marabozu, Bearish Marabozu, Hammer Pattern, Doji, Hanging Man, Shooting star, etc.

2. Double Candlestick Pattern

Double candle patterns are those patterns that are formed by the combination of two candles. Here, by looking into the two consecutive candles, the traders judge whether the price is going to be bullish, bearish or neutral.

A few popular examples of double candlestick patterns are Bullish Engulfing, Bearish Engulfing, Harami Pattern, Kicker Pattern etc.

3. Triple Candlestick Pattern

Triple candle patterns are those patterns that are formed by the combination of three candles. Here, by looking into the three consecutive candles, the traders are able to judge if the price is going to be bullish, bearish or neutral.

A few popular examples of triple candle patterns are Three White Soldiers, Morning Stars, Three Inside Down, Three Outside Down, Bearish Tri-Star, etc.

4. Multi Candlestick Pattern

Multi candle patterns are those patterns that are formed by a combination of four or more candles. Here, by looking into the four or more consecutive candles, the traders are able to judge if the price may go higher, lower, or stay neutral.

A few popular examples of the Multi candlestick patterns are Bullish Hikkake, Bearish Hikkake, Bullish Three Line Strike, Mat Hold Bullish, Ladder Top, etc.

In this book, we are going to cover many Single, Double, Triple and Multi candlestick patterns and discuss how they work along with how to trade these candlestick patterns.

A Few Important Points to Note regarding the candlestick patterns:

1. The Candle colour alone doesn't always mean bullishness or bearishness. The structure of the candle, i.e. its body and wick size, along with the position where the candle is formed, helps to identify the true nature of the candle. A red candle can also be bullish in nature and vice-versa. This is what we are going to discuss in the book.
2. The formation of Candlestick patterns at suitable levels like support, resistance level, or start or end of uptrend or downtrend helps to further confirm the bullish or bearish trade.
3. Trading candlestick patterns along with the combination of other suitable chart patterns, technical indicators and market conditions gives the best results.

SUPPORT AND RESISTANCE

Before we jump into the realm of various candlestick patterns, let us first discuss the concept of most basic yet most crucial concept of all, Support and Resistance levels. This concept tells us the behaviour of the market participants and how they perceive the prices of security at certain levels.

Throughout this book, we are going to use the terminologies of Support and Resistance. Therefore, it is important that you first understand what exactly they are and how they work so that you can relate to them correctly wherever required.

Fig. Support And Resistance Levels

What are Support Levels?

The support level is a point in the security that tries to prevent the price from declining further. This is the level where the price may pause or likely reverse upwards due to the strong buying pressure present in the market.

The basic psychology behind the support level is that the buyers interpret these zones as a good buying opportunity and buy the security leading to an increase in its price. As the price increases, more participants might buy the security, which can lead to a further increase in the price.

When the price of the security decreases and reaches near a support level, the price is expected to reverse upwards. Thus, you can consider entering a long position in the security when the price is near the support level and keep a stop loss a few points below the entry.

Fig. Support Level

Characteristics of Supports

Here are the key characteristics of Support while looking into the charts:

- Supports are those points or levels below which the market finds difficult to fall. They can also be said as a point of inflection between buyers and sellers.
- Support is also the point of maximum demand from buyers, and even the sellers exit their selling positions from the market.
- The buyers have a higher say in deciding the levels of support in the market. These levels can also be said to be the mainstay for buyers.
- Support, if breached, sees a quick sell-off in the market, and then the next level of support becomes a point of contention.
- If the levels of support hold in the market, then fresh longs can be initiated, and generally, these trades have good risk-to-reward ratios.

What are Resistance Levels?

The resistance level is a point in the security that tries to prevent the price from increasing further. This is the level where the price will pause or likely reverse downwards due to the strong selling pressure present in the market.

The basic psychology behind the resistance level is that the sellers interpret these zones as a good selling opportunity and sell the security, leading to a decrease in its price. As the price decreases, more participants might sell the security, which can lead to a further decrease in the price.

When the price of the security increases and reaches a resistance level, the price is expected to reverse downwards. Thus, you can consider entering a short position in the security when the price is near the resistance level and keep a stop loss a few points above the entry.

Fig. Resistance Level

Characteristics of Resistances

Here are the key characteristics of Resistance while looking at the charts:

- Resistances are the levels that are defended by sellers. And the market finds it difficult to go beyond that level. It is a tussle point between buyers and sellers.
- Maximum selling pressure comes from sellers at this point, and even the buyers start to exit their long positions at these levels
- If the levels of Resistance are breached in the market, we could see a massive upward move in the market, up to the next resistance levels.

- Resistances can also be called points where fresh short positions can be initiated in the market with a good risk-to-reward ratio.

Breakout of Support and Resistance Levels

While the price tends to reverse from the support and resistance level, sometimes, it tends to break beyond these levels. In such situations, the roles of support and resistance get reversed.

When the price of the security breaks below the support level, it indicates that the buying pressure has been dominated by the selling pressure in security. In this scenario, one can consider entering a short position in the security while placing a stoploss a few points above the entry.

Fig. Support becomes Resistance

Similarly, when the price of the security breaks above the resistance level, it indicates that the selling pressure has been dominated by the buying pressure in security. In this scenario, one can consider entering a long position in the security while placing a stop loss a few points below the entry.

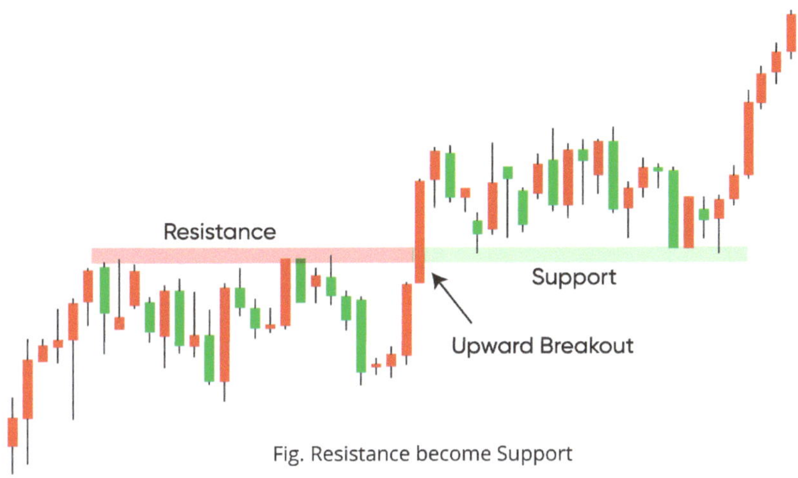

Fig. Resistance become Support

How do we plot support and resistance levels?

There are many ready-made indicators like support and resistance channels, pivot points and Fibonacci retracement that can help you plot the support and resistance levels. However, the traditional way of doing so is by plotting the historical price movements.

Marking the support and resistance levels is quite simple. All you need to do is mark the points in the security where the prices have reversed in the opposite direction of the prior trend. After these points are plotted out, draw a horizontal line across these points, which represents the support and resistance levels.

Fig. Plotting Historical Swings to Identify Support And Resistance

If the price of the security is trading above the line drawn, the line is considered to be a support level. Conversely, if the price is trading below the line drawn, the line is considered to be a resistance level.

The reliability of support and resistance lines increases as the price of the security bounces back from a specific level multiple times. It's also worth noting that support and resistance lines drawn on longer timeframes are more reliable than those drawn on shorter timeframes.

When looking into bullish and bearish candlestick patterns, we'll also discuss the location where these candles are formed and how the formation of these patterns near the significant support or resistance level further confirms the direction of the trades.

UNDERSTANDING STOP-LOSS

Another crucial concept that we are going to use throughout this book is the concept of Stop Loss and where to place it while executing various trades. Before moving forward, let us also discuss this concept.

When most of the traders are busy deciding when to enter and exit security, there's one point that they most easily overlook. And it is stop-loss. Although 'stop-loss' might sound a little complicated to beginners, however, it is really simple to understand.

What is a Stop Loss?

Stop loss is a very powerful tool available to traders and investors to limit their losses. It is an advance order to exit the shares if the share price reaches a particular price point. Therefore, it helps in exiting the trades in unfavourable market scenarios. Stop-loss can be used for both short-term and long-term but is mostly effectively used by Intraday and short-term traders.

For example, let's say that you bought 1000 shares of a company ABC at Rs 100. However, you do not want to lose more than 5% of your money in case the trade doesn't work out as expected for any reason. Here, you can put a stop loss to automatically sell your shares if its price falls below Rs 95.

Therefore, by putting a stop loss, you are limiting your losses. You are exiting the position at a 5% loss and avoiding the scenario in case the trade might turn out badly and the share price falls heavily (say 10%, 15% or 30%), resulting in bigger losses for you.

Advantages of using a stop loss

Here are a few of the top reasons to use a stop loss

1. **Cutting your losses correctly:** Stop loss helps you cut your losses and hedges you against a big loss. You are exiting a trade by booking a small loss as the trade didn't go in your favour.
2. **Automation:** A stop loss helps to automate your Exit process. A stop loss will be automatically triggered in case stock touches a specific price.
3. **Maintaining 'Risk to Reward':** It's really important to maintain risk and reward while trading. You should be stubborn with your Risk to reward. For example, you should aim to book at least 10 points of profit if you're keeping a stop loss of 10 points and hence maintaining a risk reward of at least 1:1. Stop loss helps in maintaining a risk-to-reward ratio based on how much risk traders are willing to take as stop loss, vs how much target profit they should aim for.
4. **Promoting discipline:** It's really important to detach yourself from market emotions. If trade is not going as how you planned, you should have the discipline to book losses and plan the next trade. A stop loss helps you to adhere to your strategy and promotes disciplined trading.

What Should you do if your stop loss is hit?

In general, your stop loss should hit when your view is wrong. However, in case your view is intact and your stop loss got hit just because of market volatility, you can enter the trade again. Nonetheless, make sure not to re-enter the same trade multiple times if it is not going in your favour, as it simply means that it might not be your day, and you may incur multiple losses.

In addition, if your stop loss is hit, be comfortable and do not get much detached from the trade or losses. While setting the stop loss, you already knew how much risk you were willing to take if that stop loss got hit.

Finally and most importantly, make sure to keep your stop loss at the appropriate place so that you do not get prematurely stopped out of the trade. Throughout the book, I have discussed where you should keep your stop loss when you are trading different chart patterns to help you make better trades and maintain a good risk-to-reward.

BULLISH SINGLE CANDLESTICK PATTERN

Bullish Single Candlestick Patterns are those candle patterns that are made by just a single candle and are inherently bullish by nature, i.e. suggest that the prices may go higher after these candle patterns are formed. Now, let us discuss these candle patterns and understand how they are identified.

1) Bullish Marubozu

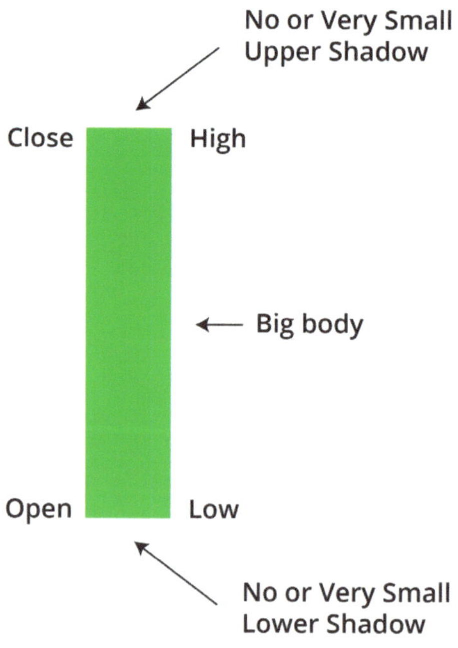

Fig. Bullish Marubozu

The term Marubozu in Japanese refers to a 'Shaved Head' or 'Bald'. In technical analysis, Marubozu is a single candlestick pattern that comprises a large body with little to no upper or lower wick.

A bullish Marubozu pattern is a large-bodied green candlestick, and the appearance of this pattern suggests a strong bullishness in the market.

This pattern works best when it forms at the end of the downtrend or near a support level, indicating a shift in the market sentiment. At the same time, this pattern also works if it appears during an existing uptrend.

How to Trade Bullish Marubozu?

Before considering entering a trade using Bullish Marubozu, make sure that the market conditions favour the candlestick pattern, i.e. it is formed at the end of a downtrend or near the support level. Once the favourable conditions are met, you proceed to enter a trade in the security.

One can enter a long position in the security when the next candle starts trading above the Marubozu. Simultaneously, one should place a stop-loss at the close or the lowest point of the Marubozu pattern or at the immediate support level below it.

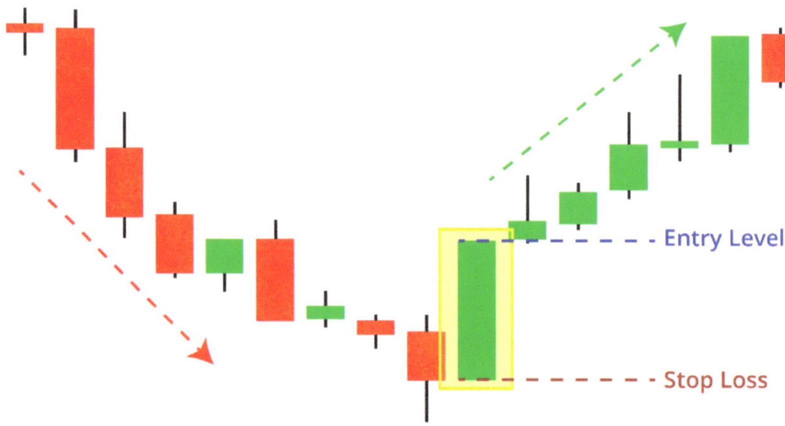

Fig. Bullish Marubozu

2) Hammer Pattern

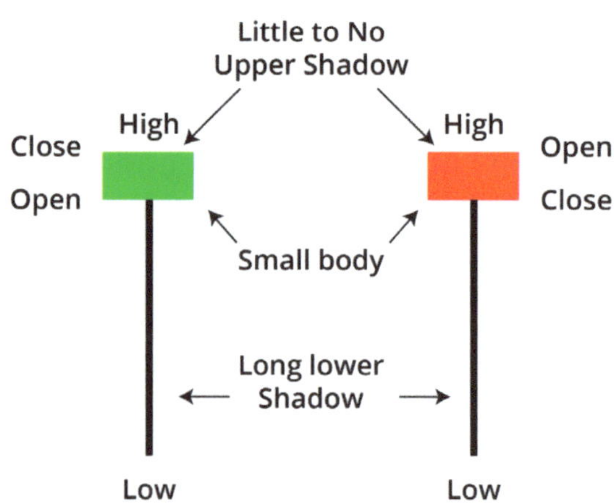

Fig. Hammer

Hammer is one of the most popular single bullish candle patterns. A hammer pattern is a reversal pattern that is spotted at the bottom of a downtrend. This single candlestick pattern comprises of a small body, no upper wick and a large lower wick, which should be at least twice the size of the body.

The colour of the body of the candle can either be green or red. This pattern suggests that the sellers were in control earlier, but the buyers have now entered and overcome the selling pressure in the market.

How to Trade Hammer Pattern?

Once a hammer pattern has been identified, look for further confirmation that can help you validate a trade along with the pattern. The appearance of the hammer pattern near a significant support level is the best scenario for this pattern to work.

One can enter a long position in the security when the price starts trading above the candlestick pattern. Simultaneously, one should place a stop-loss at the low of the hammer pattern.

Fig. Hammer Pattern

3) Inverted Hammer

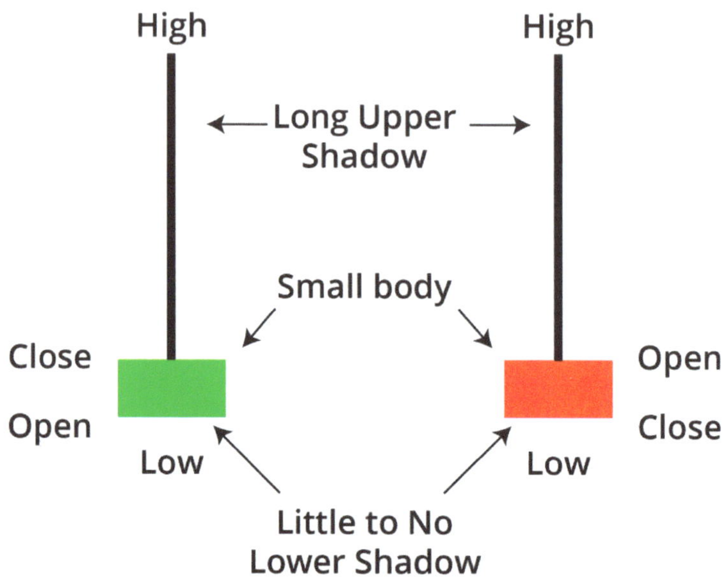

Fig. Inverted Hammer

An inverted hammer pattern is a reversal pattern that looks like a flipped hammer pattern. It is also a reversal pattern that comprises a small body, no lower wick and a large upper wick twice the size of the body.

The colour of the body of the candle can either be green or red, but it doesn't make much difference as it has a very small body.

This pattern suggests that the buyers entered the market during the selling pressure, and the price paused to move downwards. After a downtrend, the formation of an inverted hammer is a bullish pattern because it shows that bulls are now testing the power of the bears.

How to Trade Inverted Hammer Pattern?

When an inverted hammer appears, wait for the price to move higher before entering a trade for confirmation. If the next candles are not green or doesn't trade higher than the inverted hammer pattern, it is a failed attempt by the buyers to overthrow the sellers.

One can enter a long position in the security when the price starts trading above the green candle that appears after the inverted hammer candlestick pattern. Simultaneously, one should place a stop-loss at the low of the inverted hammer pattern while executing this trade.

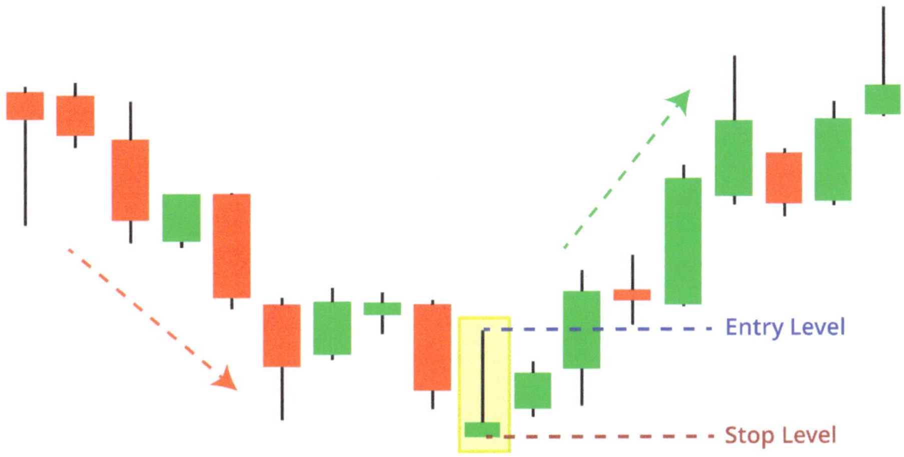

Fig. Inverted Hammer Pattern

4) Dragonfly Doji

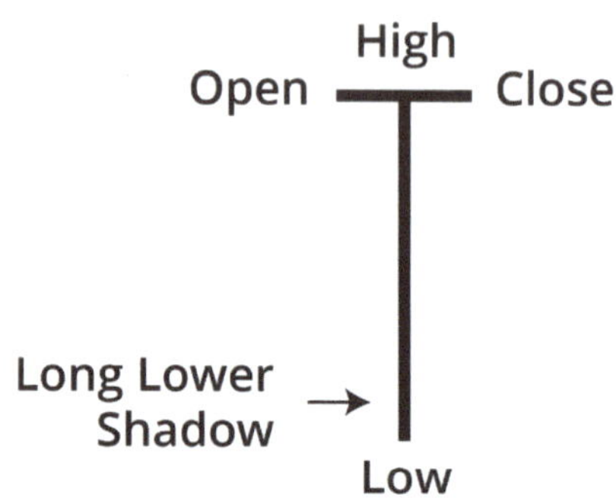

Fig. Dragonfly Doji

A dragonfly doji is a neutral to bullish reversal pattern. This pattern consists of a very long lower wick with little to no body and no upper wick, which creates a 'T' Pattern.

This pattern suggests that there was earlier strong selling pressure in the market, but the buyers entered and pushed the price to its opening level, causing an equilibrium between the buyers and the sellers in the market. If the next candle is green and rises above the last one, it confirms a bullish trade.

How to Trade a Dragonfly Doji?

A dragonfly doji cannot be interpreted as a clear bullish signal, and thus, one has to look for additional confirmations to validate the potential reversal in the market.

It is recommended to go long only after the price starts trading above the dragonfly doji. Entering a long position above the doji candle helps you confirm the bullish reversal. At the same time, place a stop-loss at the low of price of the Dragonfly Doji.

Fig. Dragonfly Doji

BEARISH SINGLE CANDLESTICK PATTERN

Bearish Single Candlestick Patterns are those candle patterns that are made by just a single candle and are inherently bearish by nature, i.e. suggest that prices may go lower after these candle patterns are formed.

Now, let us discuss how these single bearish candle patterns are formed and understand how they are identified and traded.

1) Bearish Marubozu

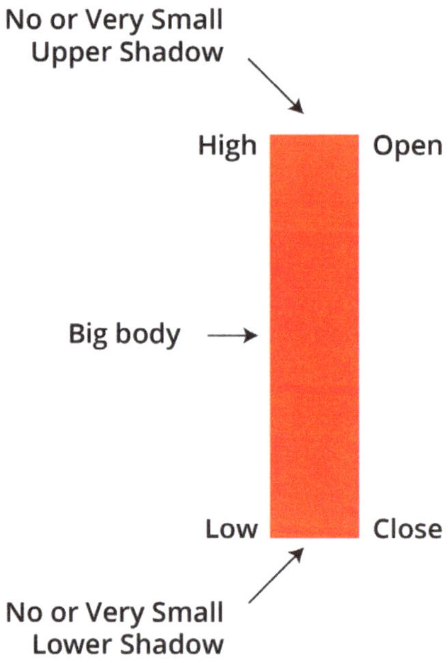

Fig. Bearish Marubozu

A bearish Marubozu pattern is a large-bodied red candlestick, and no or very small upper and lower wick or shadows are formed in this candle pattern. The appearance of this pattern suggests a strong bearishness in the market.

This pattern works best when it forms at the end of an uptrend, indicating a shift in the market sentiment. At the same time, this pattern also works if it appears during an existing downtrend.

How to Trade Bearish Marubozu?

Before considering entering a trade using bearish Marubozu, make sure that the market conditions are favouring the candlestick pattern. Here, the market can be approaching the end of an uptrend or a resistance level or already in a downtrend. Once the favourable conditions are met, you proceed to enter a trade in the security.

One can enter a short position in the security when the next candle starts trading below the Marubozu. Simultaneously, one should place a stop-loss at the top of the Marubozu pattern or at the immediate resistance level.

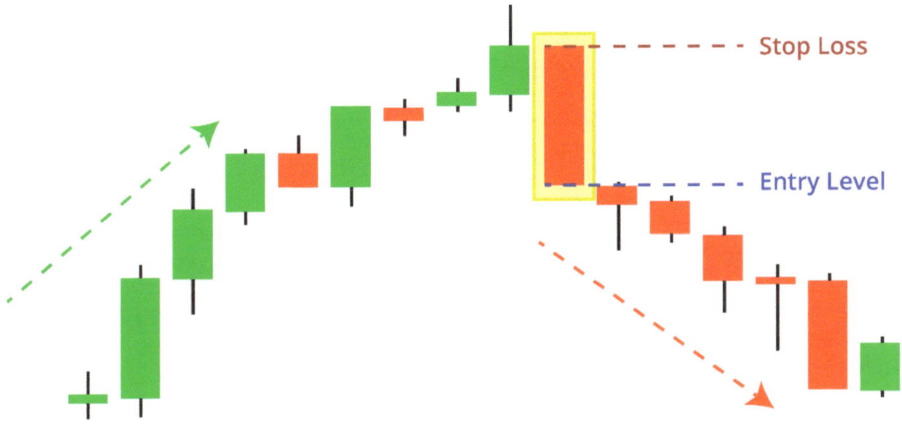

Fig. Bearish Marubozu

2) Hanging Man

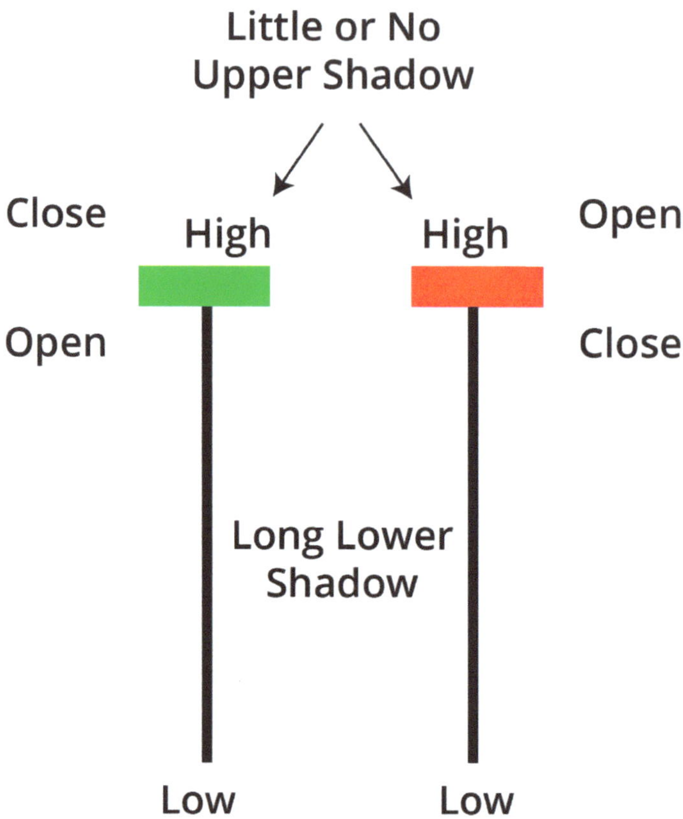

A Hanging pattern looks similar to a hammer candlestick pattern and is characterised by a small body, a long lower wick and little to no upper wick. But here, this pattern appears at the top of an uptrend and suggests a bearish reversal.

Similar to the hammer pattern, the colour of the body of the Hanging man pattern can either be green or red. This pattern suggests that the sellers entered the market during a buying pressure, though the buyers were able to push the price back up, resulting in the long lower wick.

How to Trade a Hanging Man Pattern?

Once a hanging man pattern has been identified, wait for the prices to go lower than the Hanging man candle for confirmation.

One can enter a short position in the security when the price starts trading below the hanging man pattern. The stop-loss for this trade should be placed at the high of the Hanging man pattern.

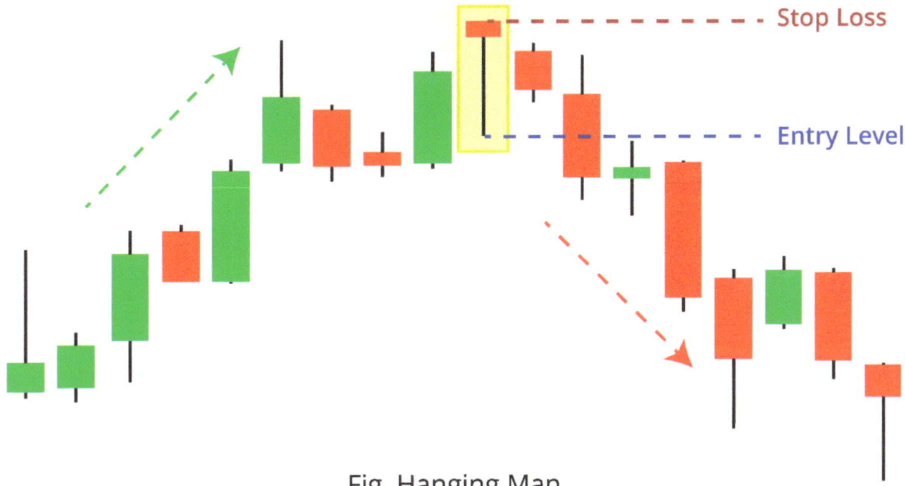

Fig. Hanging Man

3) Shooting Star

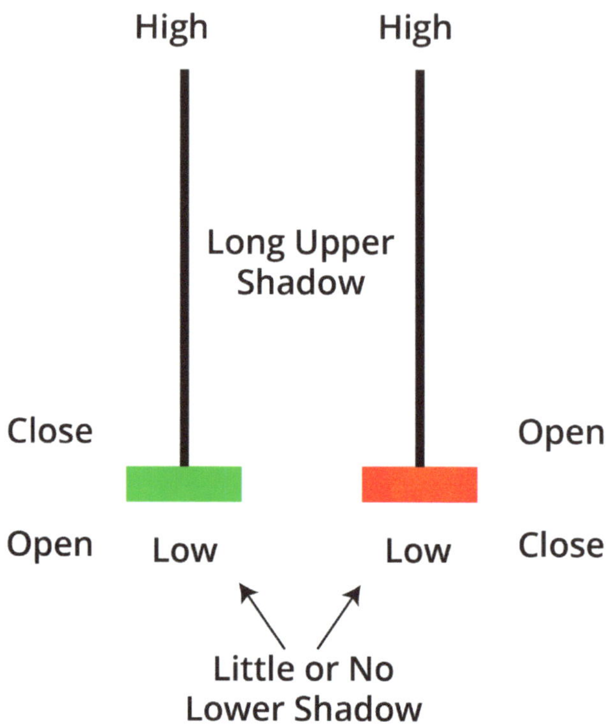

Fig. Shooting Star

A shooting star is a reversal pattern that is spotted at the top of an uptrend. This single candlestick pattern comprises of a small body, no lower wick and a large upper wick, which is at least twice the size of the body. This pattern is similar to that of an inverted hammer, except that it appears at the top of an uptrend.

The colour of the body of the candle can either be green or red in colour. This pattern suggests that the buyers were in control earlier, but now the sellers have entered and overcome the buying pressure in the market.

How to trade a Shooting Star pattern?

Once a shooting star pattern has been identified, look for further confirmation to help you validate a trade along with the pattern. The appearance of this pattern near a significant resistance level is a good scenario for this pattern to work.

One can enter a short position in the security when the price starts trading below the candlestick pattern. Simultaneously, one should place a stop-loss at the high of the pattern.

Fig. Shooting Star

4) Gravestone Doji

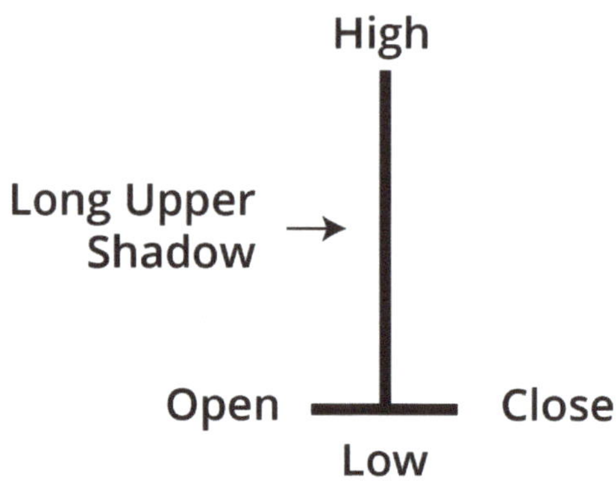

Fig. Gravestone Doji

A gravestone doji is the opposite of a dragonfly doji and it indicates neutral to bearish sentiment in the market. The gravestone doji comprises of a long upper wick with little to no body and no lower wick.

This pattern suggests that there was earlier a strong buying pressure in the market, but the sellers entered and pushed the price to its opening level, causing an equilibrium between the buyers and the sellers in the market.

How to Trade a Gravestone Doji?

Like the dragonfly doji, a gravestone doji cannot be interpreted as a clear bearish signal, and thus, one has to look for additional confirmations to validate the potential reversal in the market.

It is recommended to enter a short position after a dragonfly doji if the price starts trading below the candle pattern. At the same time, place a stop-loss at the high price of the gravestone doji.

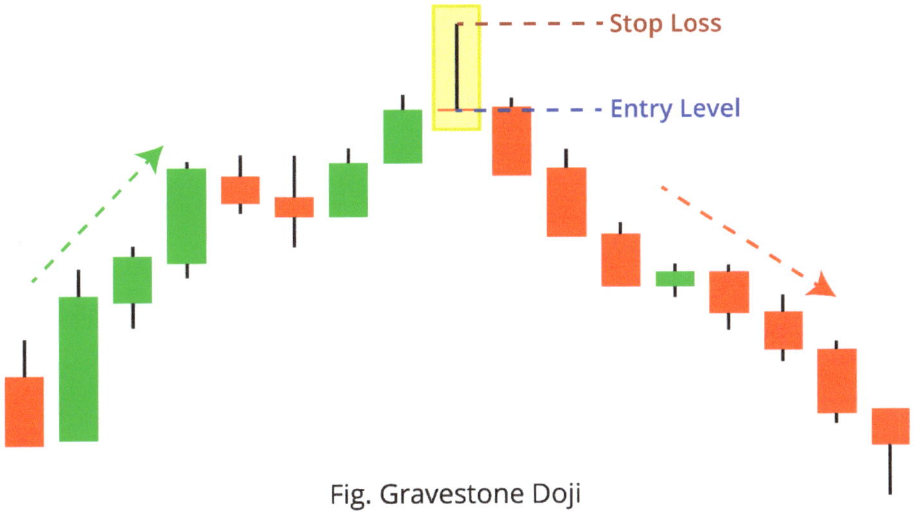

Fig. Gravestone Doji

NEUTRAL SINGLE CANDLESTICK PATTERN

We have discussed the bullish and bearish single candlestick patterns in the previous sections. However, there are certain candlesticks that indicate indecision in the market. These are known as neutral candlestick patterns.

The Neutral candlestick patterns suggest a lack of consensus between buyers and sellers. In this section, we will be discussing these neutral single candlestick patterns in detail.

1) Neutral Doji

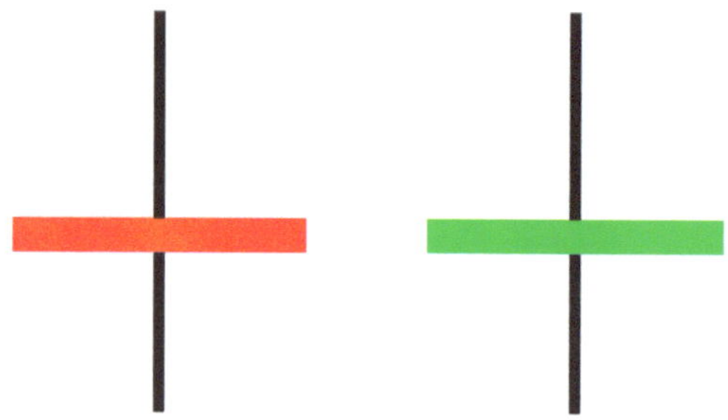

Fig. Netural Doji

A doji is a single candlestick pattern that opens and closes almost on the same level. Thus, it has little to no body and small upper and lower wicks.

This pattern indicates an indecision between the buyers and sellers. This pattern can indicate a potential trend reversal after a significant uptrend or a downtrend and can also be used as a continuation pattern. However, you have to wait for a confirmation.

For example, if the market is in an uptrend and a doji is formed, it means that the market is taking a halt. Based on the next candle, it can either reverse or continue the existing trend. If the next candle starts trading below the candle, it means that the market may reverse and go downwards after the formation of the Doji pattern. On the other hand, if the next candle starts trading above the Doji pattern, it means that the current uptrend may continue. A similar is true in the vice-versa case.

2) Long-Legged Doji

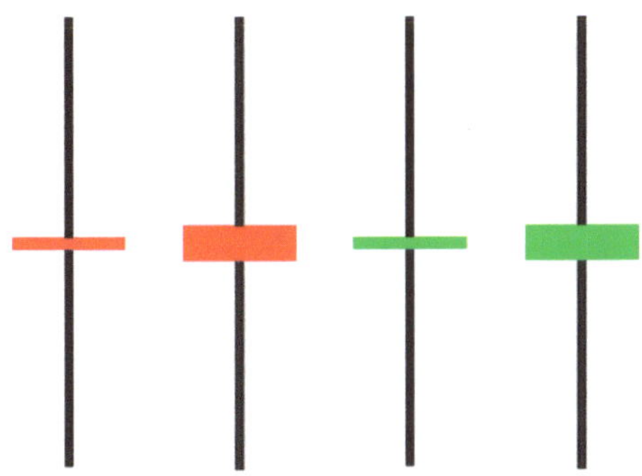

Fig. Long Legged Doji

A long-legged doji is a candlestick pattern that resembles a doji. However, this pattern signifies that both buyers and sellers were trying to push the price in their favour, leading to significant volatility during the session.

This battle between buyers and sellers causes huge volatility during the session, resulting in the long upper and lower wicks. Towards the end of the session, the price eventually closes almost at the same level where it opened, resulting in a small or non-existent body.

This pattern can indicate a potential trend reversal after a significant uptrend or a downtrend and can also be used as a continuation pattern, depending on what the evidence for the trend arises.

3) Spinning Top

Fig. Spinning Top

A spinning top is a neutral candlestick pattern that comprises a small body and a large upper and lower wick. Here, the body of the candle can either be red or green in colour.

This pattern indicates that there was a movement in the price of the security in both directions, but the session ended without buyers or sellers gaining any significant control.

This pattern can indicate a potential trend reversal after a significant uptrend or a downtrend and can also be used as a continuation pattern.

If we compare Spinning tops with Dojis, both are neutral candle patterns and represent indecision in the market and potential reversal after a trend. However, the Spinning top has longer upper and lower shadows compared to the Dojis, which has shorter upper and lower shadows.

4) High Wave Pattern

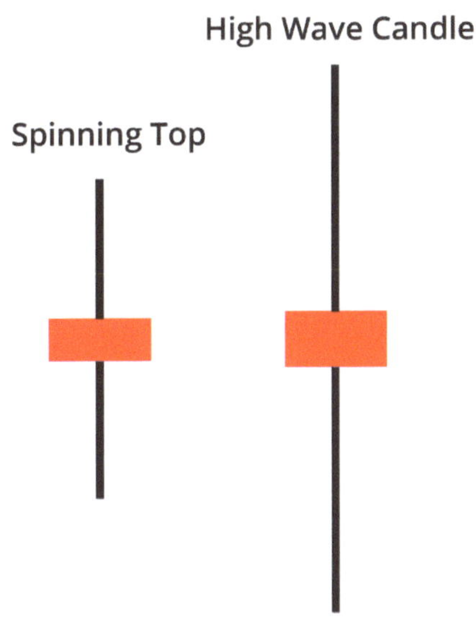

Fig. High Wave Candle

The High wave pattern is a neutral candlestick pattern that looks similar to the spinning top pattern. It comprises a small body, and the upper and lower wicks are larger than that of a spinning top. Here, the body of the candle can either be red or green in colour.

Like the spinning top, this pattern also indicates that there was a movement in the price of the security in both directions, but the session closed without buyers or sellers gaining control.

This pattern can indicate a potential trend reversal after a significant uptrend or a downtrend and can also be used as a continuation pattern.

How to trade the Neutral Candlestick Patterns?

As the neutral candlestick patterns indicate indecision in the market, one has to decide their trades based on the direction of the next candle.

After a downtrend, if a neutral candlestick pattern appears, wait for another green candle to appear to confirm the potential bullish trend reversal. One can place a long position in the security if the price starts trading above the high of the green candle and keep a stop loss at the low of the neutral patterns.

Fig. Neutral Candlestick at the end of a Downtrend

After an uptrend, if a neutral candlestick pattern appears, wait for another red candle to appear to confirm the potential trend reversal. One can place a short position in the security if the price starts trading below the low of the red candle and place a stop loss at the high of the neutral patterns.

Fig. Neutral Candlestick at the end of an Uptrend

After the appearance of a neutral candlestick, if the price of security continues to move in the same direction as the prior trend, it may be a good idea to take a trade based on that trend as a continuation.

For example, if the security is moving upwards, you could consider entering a long position.

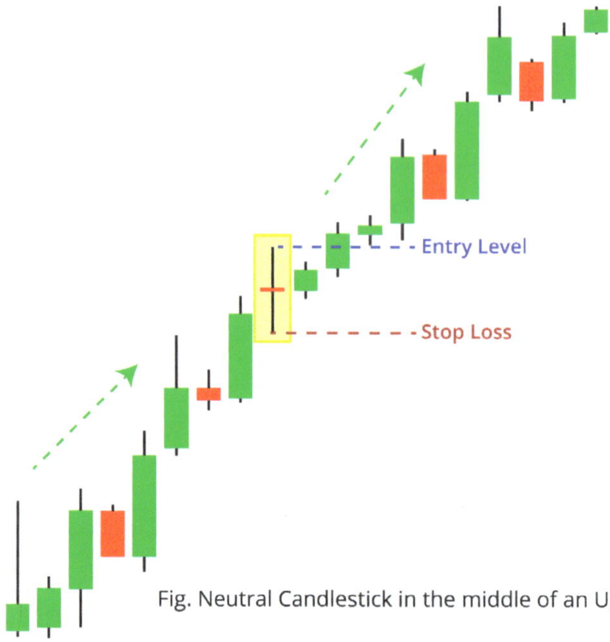

Fig. Neutral Candlestick in the middle of an Uptrend

On the other hand, if it's moving downwards, you may consider entering a short position.

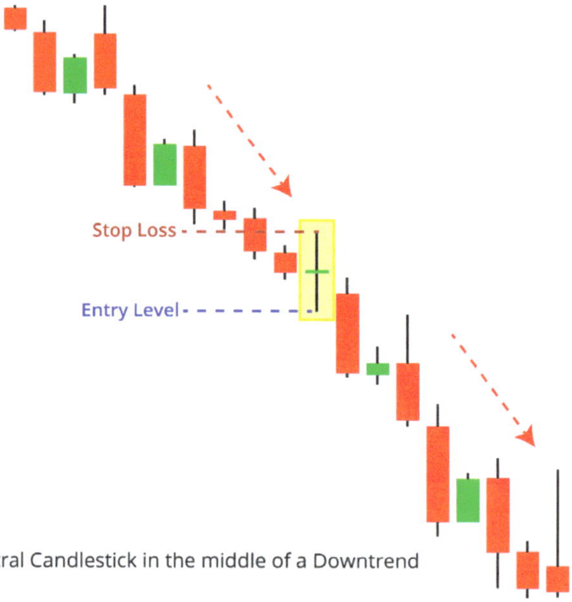

Fig. Neutral Candlestick in the middle of a Downtrend

BULLISH TWO CANDLESTICK PATTERN

In the Bullish Two Candlestick Pattern, we'll discuss those candle patterns that inherently represent bullishness. This pattern consists of two consecutive candles, and here, you need to look into both the first and second candles to get confirmation of the pattern.

1) Bullish Engulfing

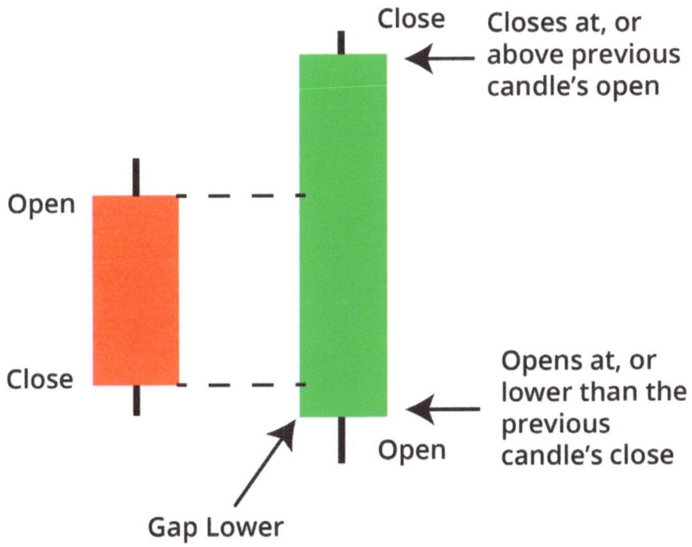

Fig. Bullish Engulfing

A bullish engulfing is a candlestick pattern that is formed when a large green candle completely covers the body of the previous red candle. Basically, the second candle completely engulfs the first candle. Here, the size of the wicks in this pattern is not relevant as long as the engulfing has occurred.

The appearance of this pattern indicates that the buyers have overpowered the sellers in the market. A good case scenario to trade this pattern is when it appears after a downtrend, as it indicates a potential reversal. At the same time, this pattern can also be used during an existing uptrend.

How to Trade a Bullish Engulfing Pattern?

After the appearance of the bullish engulfing pattern, enter a long position when the price of the security starts trading above the pattern. A stop-loss for this pattern should be placed below the low of the bullish engulfing pattern,

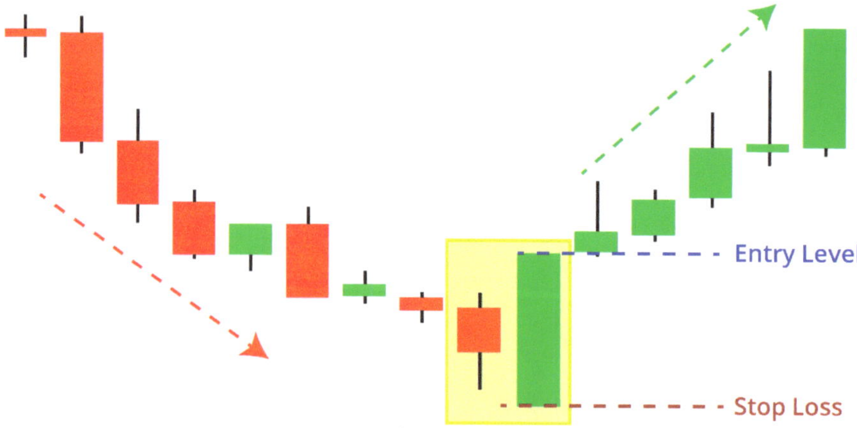

Fig. Bullish Engulfing

2) Bullish Harami

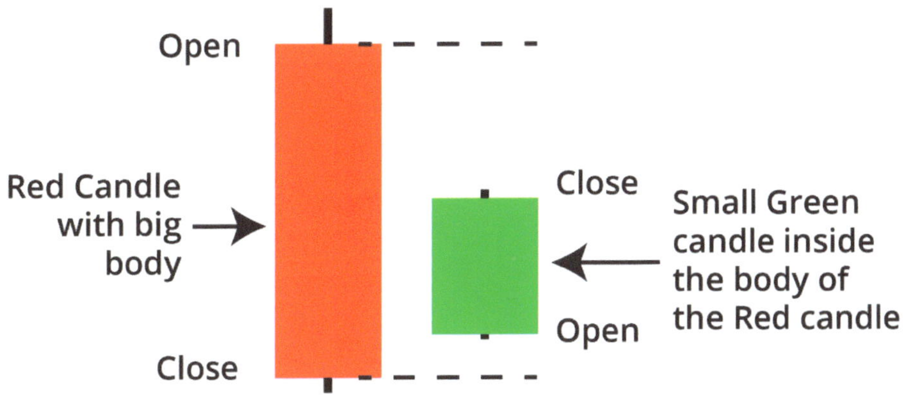

Fig. Bullish Harami

The word 'Harami' means 'Pregnant' in Japanese. The harami pattern is also based on this word, as its structure resembles that of a pregnant woman.

A bullish harami pattern is a reversal pattern that constitutes a small green candle that forms within the body of the previous larger red candle. Moreover, it is similar to the mirror image of an engulfing candle, with colours reversed.

In this pattern, the length of the wicks is not very relevant. However, it is preferred that the wicks of the smaller green candle be inside the larger red candle.

This pattern suggests that the sellers are losing control of the downtrend, and the buyers are starting to gain momentum in the market.

How to Trade a Bullish Harami Pattern?

After the formation of a bullish harami pattern, enter a long position when the price of the security starts trading above the opening price of the red candle. The stop-loss should be placed below the closing price of the red candle.

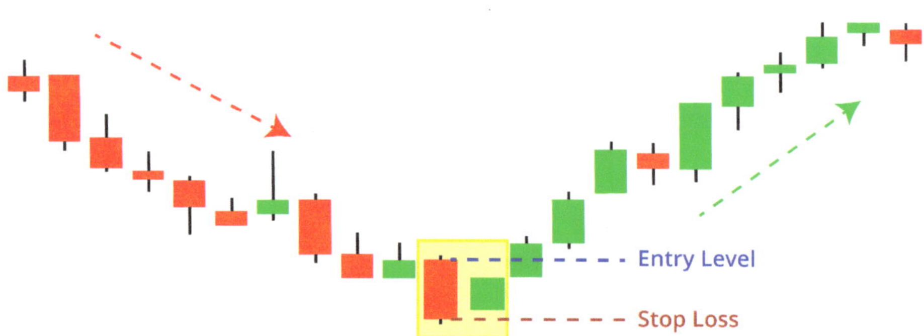

Fig. Bullish Harami pattern

3) Bullish Harami Cross

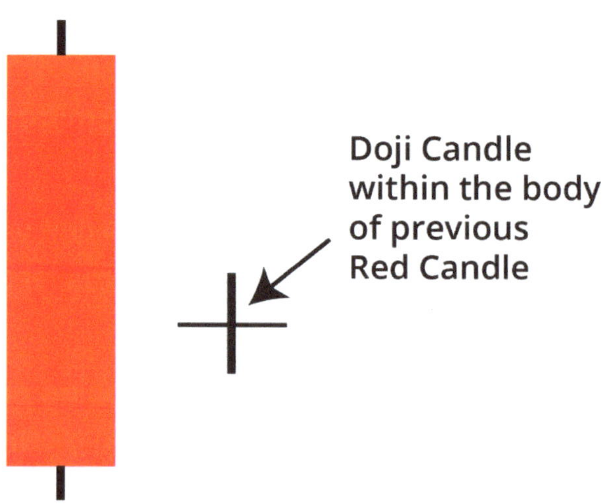

Fig. Bullish Harami Cross

A bullish harami cross is another reversal pattern that bears a resemblance to a harami pattern. This pattern consists of a doji candle within the body of the previous red candle.

The occurrence of this pattern during a downtrend indicates the potential loss of momentum from sellers and buyers gaining control of the market. However, the strength of the buyers is only confirmed once the price of security starts trading above the opening price of the red candle.

How to Trade a Bullish Harami Cross Pattern?

The execution of a Bullish Harami Cross trade is similar to that of a bullish harami pattern. Here, you can enter a long position when the price of the security starts trading above the opening price of the red candle, with the stop-loss placed at the closing price of the red candle.

Fig. Bullish Harami Cross

4) Bullish Piercing Line

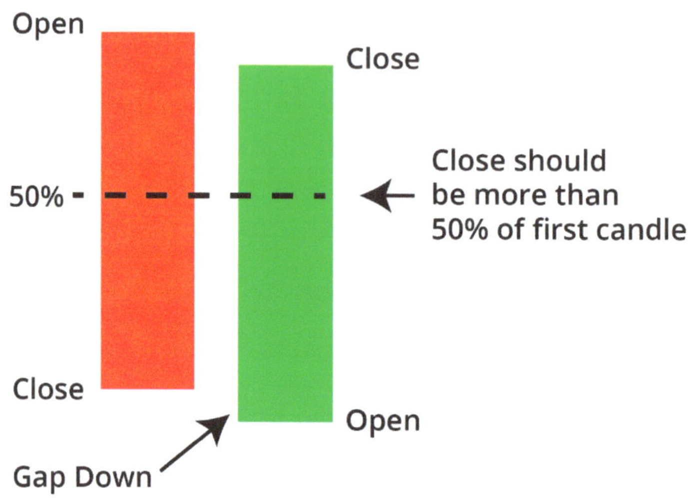

Fig. Bullish Piercing Line

The piercing pattern is a bullish reversal pattern that consists of a large red candle followed by a gap-down green candle. The green candle ends up closing above the mid-point and below the closing of the previous red candle.

The red candle in this pattern during a downtrend suggests that sellers had a strong grip on the downward movement. But the large green candle closing above mid point of the previous candle after the gap-down suggests a strong inflow of buyers, indicating a potential trend reversal.

How to Trade a Bullish Piercing Line?

One can enter a long position using the Bullish Piercing Line pattern when the price of the security starts trading above the green candle. The stop-loss for this trade should be placed at the low of the piercing line candlestick pattern.

Fig. Piercing Line Pattern

5) Bullish Kicker Pattern

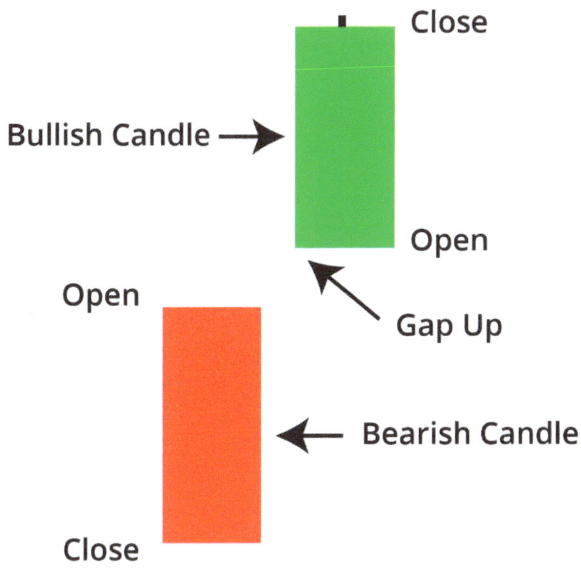

Fig. Bullish Kicker

The bullish kicker is a two-candlestick reversal pattern that constitutes a red candle followed by a gap-up green candle. Here, the green candle should open above the body of the red candle.

This red candle in the pattern suggests that the sellers were in control of the security. However, the sudden appearance of the green candle indicates that the buyers have aggressively entered and pushed the price higher.

Furthermore, if you find this bullish kicker pattern in an uptrend, it may mean that the uptrend may continue, and there's still strength left in the buyers.

How to Trade a Bullish Kicker Pattern?

One can enter a long position in the security when the price starts trading above the high of the kicker pattern. The stop-loss for this trade should be below the opening price of the red candle.

Fig. Bullish Kicker Pattern

6) Tweezer Bottom

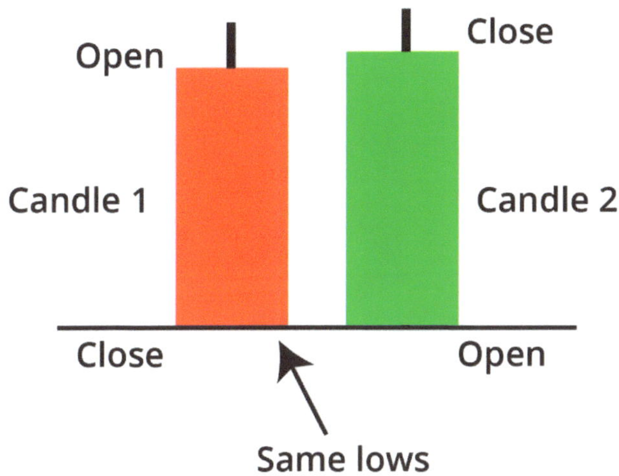

Fig. Tweezer Bottom

The Tweezer bottom is a bullish reversal pattern that consists of two candlesticks with the same lows. The first candle should be a red candle that is part of the existing downtrend, and the second candle should be a green candle that has the same low as the preceding red candle.

This pattern suggests that the sellers have been exhausted and the buyers have entered the security. It is more suited if the pattern appears near a significant support level.

How to Trade a Tweezer Bottom Pattern?

One can enter a long position in the security when the price starts trading above the high of the green candle. The stop-loss for this trade is at the low of the two-candle pattern.

Fig. Tweezer Bottom

7) Bullish Counterattack

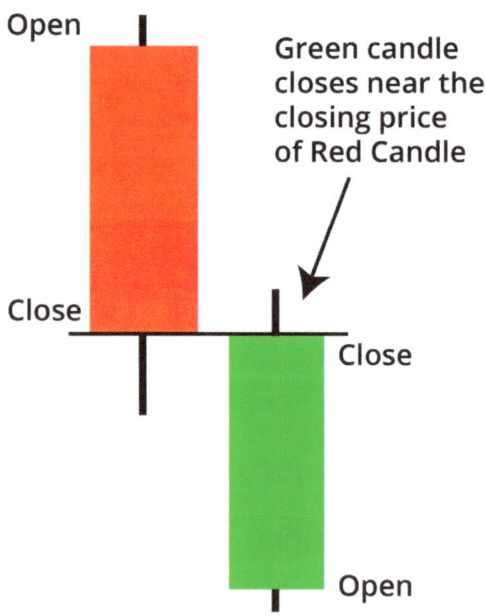

Fig. Bullish Counterattack

The bullish counterattack is a reversal pattern that constitutes a red candle followed by a gap-down green candle that closes near the closing price of the previous red candle.

This red candle and gap down indicate that the sellers were in control of the price of security. However, the next green candle suggests the sudden entrance of the buyers and that the selling pressure is weakening in the security.

How to Trade a Bullish Counterattack Pattern?

One can enter a long position in the security when the price starts trading above the high of the green candle of the pattern. Simultaneously, one can place a stop-loss below the low of the green candle.

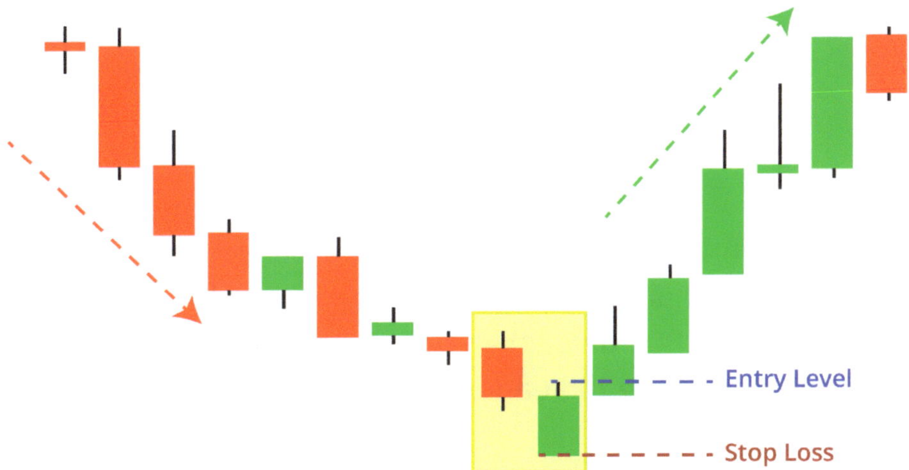

Fig. Bullish Counterattack

8) Upside Thrust

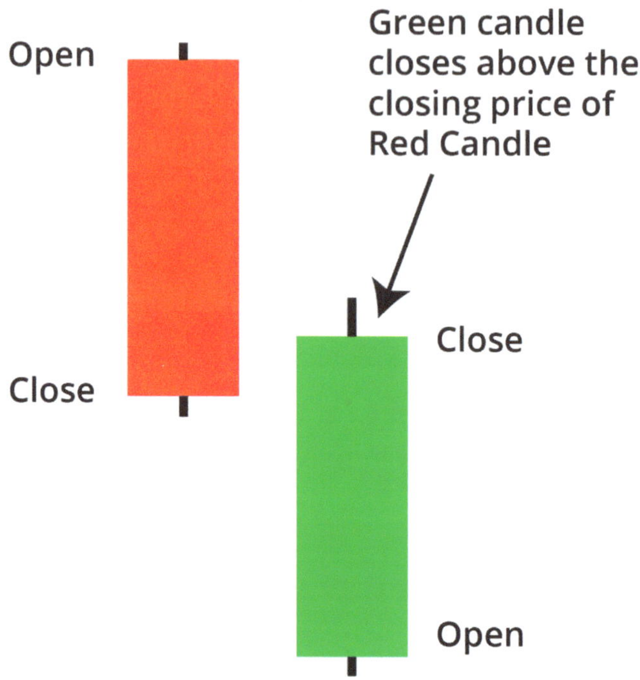

Fig. Upside Thrust

This pattern looks similar to that of a bullish counterattack pattern. It comprises a red candle followed by a gap-down green candle. But here, the green candle closes above the closing price of the red candle and below the midpoint of the red candle.

The Upside Thrust pattern suggests that buyers are intervening in the selling pressure and trying to push the price up. This pattern indicates a potential bearish continuation as well as a potential bullish reversal based on the overall context of the market and how the next candle comes up.

How to Trade an Upside Thrust Pattern?

As this pattern suggests a move in either direction, there are two ways one can enter a trade.

If the security is trading above the green candle, enter a long position in the security and simultaneously place a stop-loss below the low of the green candle.

Fig. Upside Thrust

If the price of the security starts trading below the low of the green candle, one can enter a short position as a bearish continuation and simultaneously place a stop-loss above the high of the green candle.

9) Rising Window

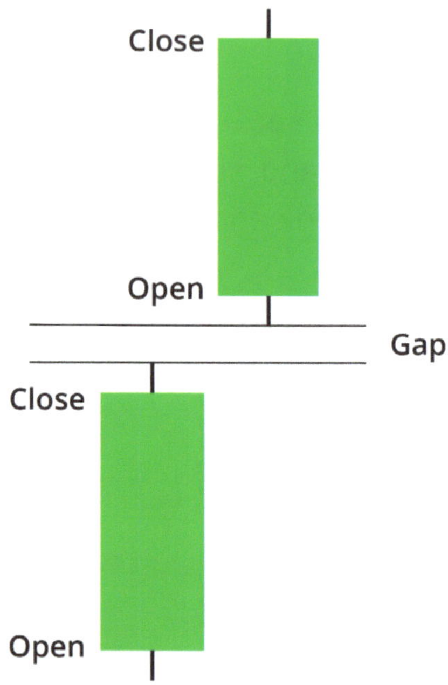

Fig. Rising Window

A Rising window is a bullish continuation pattern that comprises two consecutive green candles. Here, the high and low of the first and second green candles, respectively, are separated by a gap up opening between them.

This pattern suggests that there is strong bullish sentiment, and the buyers are willing to pay an even higher price for the security.

How to Trade a Rising Window Pattern?

After the formation of the pattern, enter a long position in the security if the price starts trading above the high of the second green candle. In general, the stop-loss for this trade should be placed at the high of the first green candle as the gap will work as support.

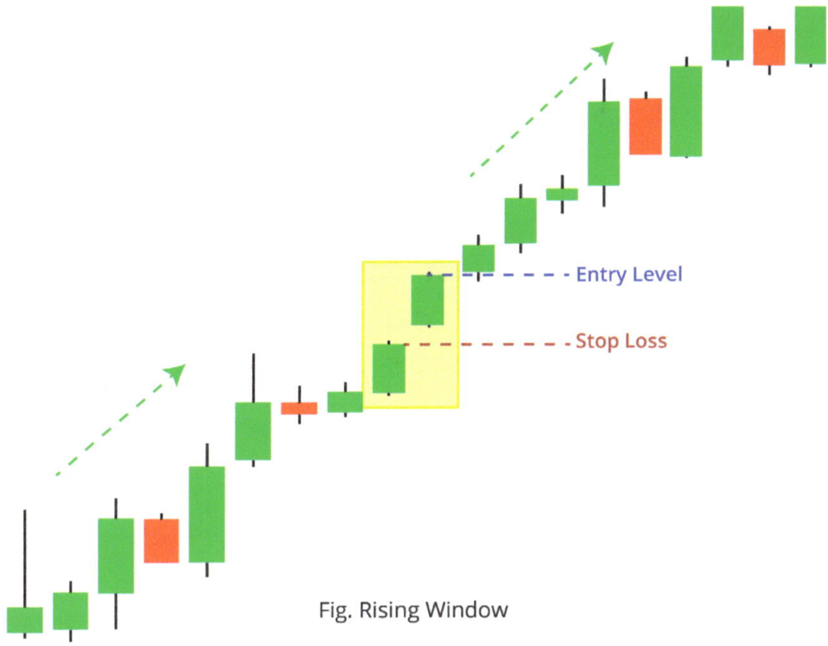

Fig. Rising Window

10) Bullish Homing Pigeon

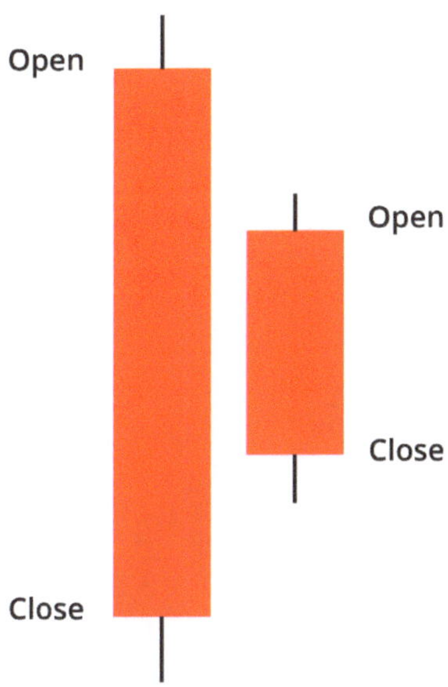

Fig. Bullish Homing Pigeon

The bullish homing pigeon is a reversal pattern that consists of two red candles, where the first candle is a large red candle and the second candle is a smaller red candle that fits within the body of the first candle.

This pattern can act as both a bullish reversal pattern as well as a bearish continuation pattern. For a Bullish reversal, the appearance of this pattern near a support level suggests that the sellers are losing the momentum of the security.

How to Trade a Bullish Homing Pigeon Pattern?

One can enter a long position using this pattern when the price of the security starts trading above the high of the second candle. However, a conservative trader can also wait for the price of the security to cross above the high of the first candle before entering.

The stop-loss for this trade should be placed at the low of the candlestick pattern.

Fig. Bullish Homing Pigeon

11) Bullish On Neck Pattern

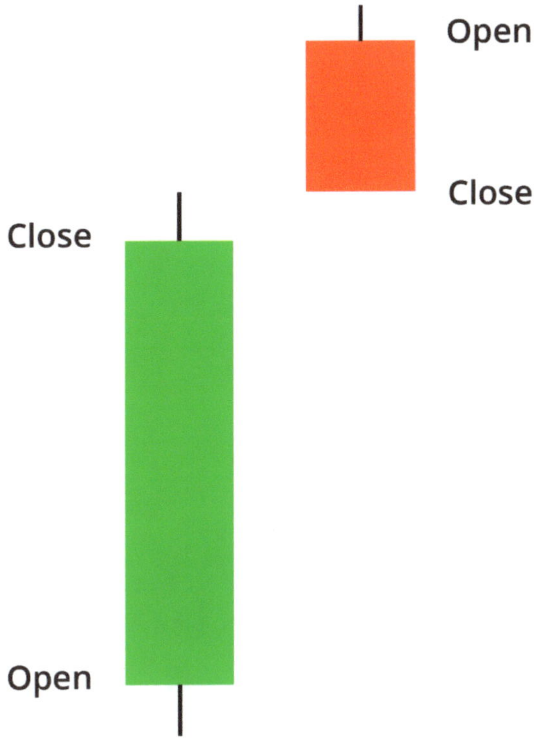

Fig . Bullish On Neck Pattern

The bullish On-Neck pattern is a continuation pattern that occurs when a large green candle is followed by a gap-up red candle that closes near the closing price of the prior green candle. The second candle should have a smaller body than the previous candle but can be in any shape.

This pattern indicates that the sellers failed to overpower the buyers in the security, and the bullish trend will likely continue further.

How to Trade a Bullish On Neck Pattern?

One can enter a long position in the security when the price starts trading above the high of the red candle of the pattern. Simultaneously, one should place a stop-loss below the low of the first green candle to avoid premature stopping out.

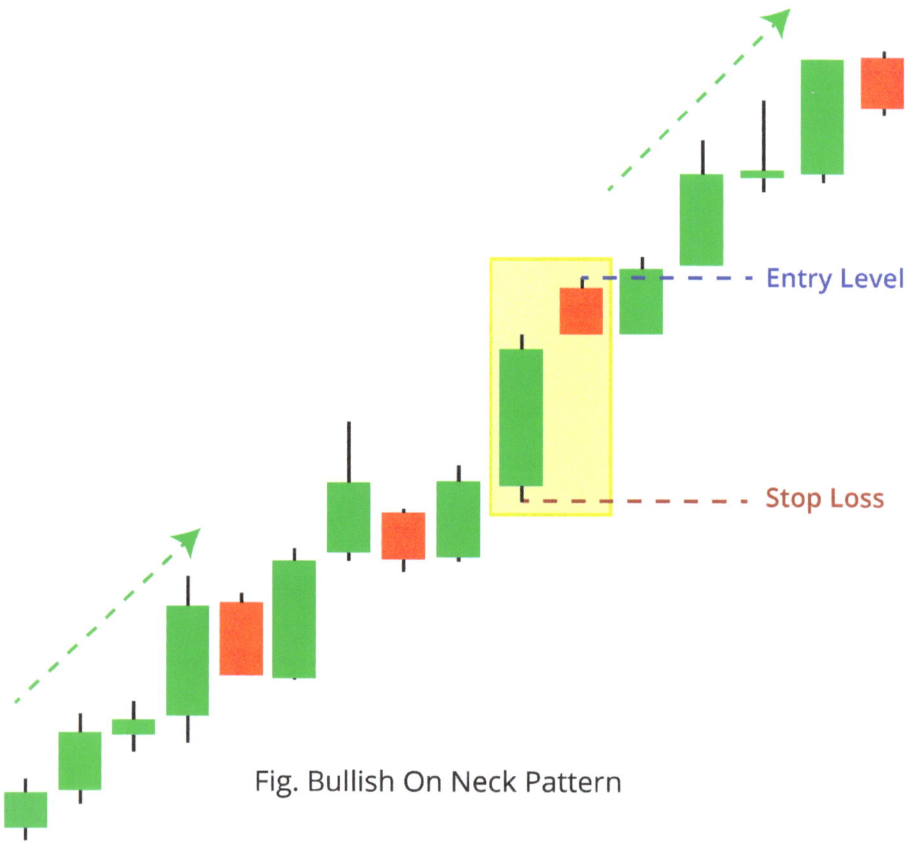

Fig. Bullish On Neck Pattern

BEARISH TWO CANDLESTICK PATTERN

In this chapter, we are going to discuss the Bearish Two Candlestick Pattern, where we will cover those candle patterns that inherently represent bearness and consist of two consecutive candlesticks. Here, you need to look into both the first and second candle to get the confirmation of the candle pattern.

1) Bearish Engulfing

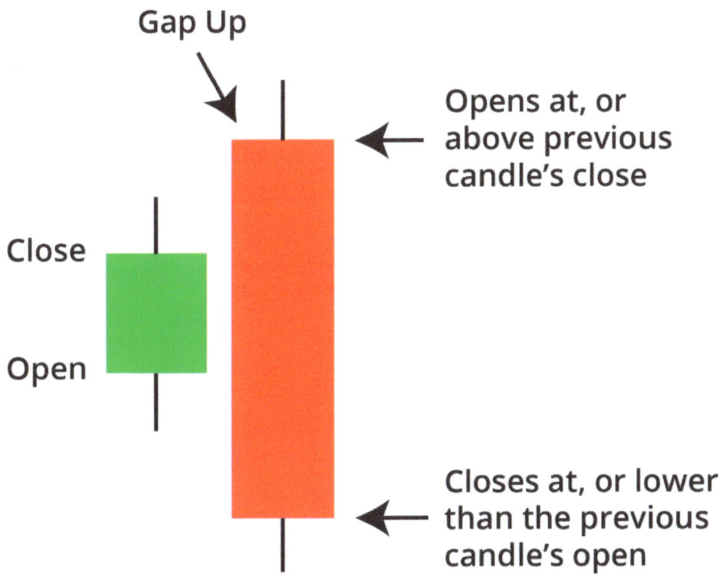

Fig. Bearish Engulfing

A bearish engulfing is a candlestick pattern that is formed when a large red candle completely covers the body of the previous green candle. The size of the wicks in this pattern is not relevant as long as the engulfing has occurred.

The appearance of this bearish engulfing pattern indicates that the sellers have overpowered the buyers in the market. The best-case scenario for this pattern to appear is during the end of an uptrend, as it indicates a potential reversal. At the same time, this pattern can also be used during an existing downtrend.

How to Trade a Bearish Engulfing Pattern?

After the appearance of the bearish engulfing pattern, enter a short position when the price of the security starts trading below the closing of this pattern. A stop-loss for this pattern should be placed above the high of the bearish engulfing pattern.

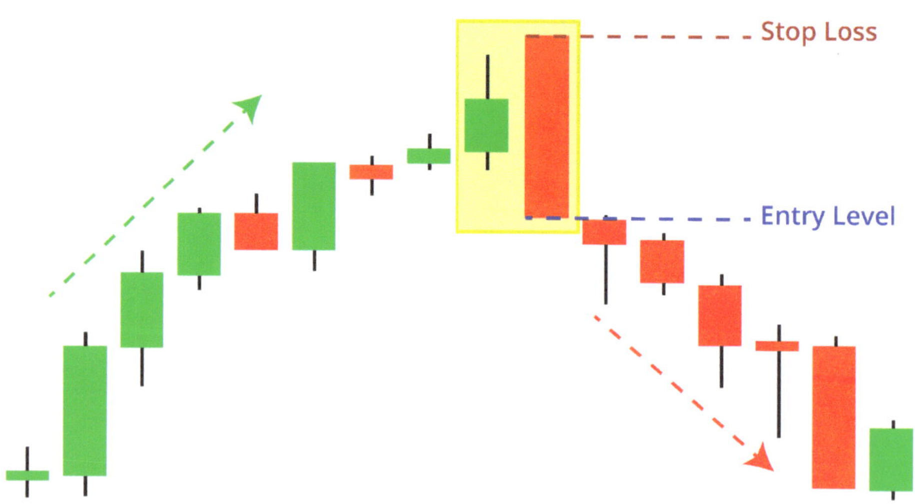

Fig. Bearish Engulfing

2) Bearish Harami

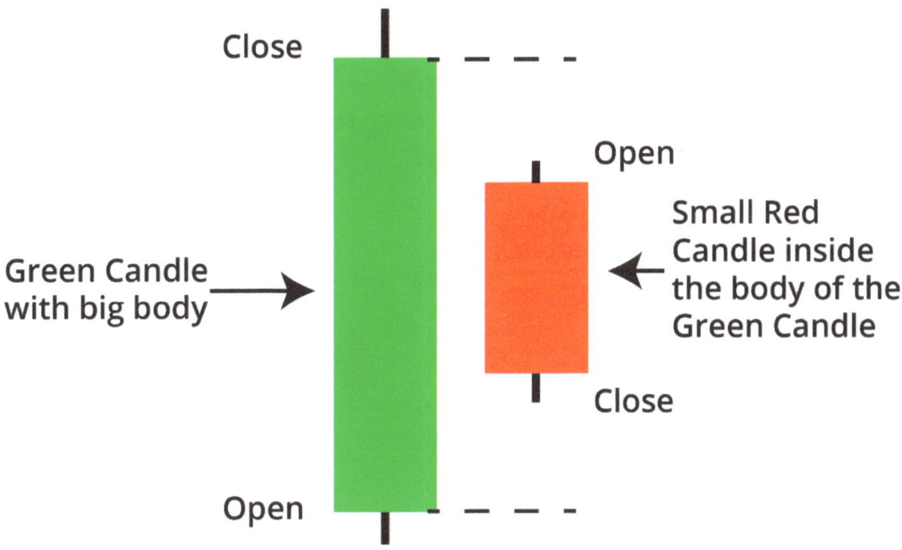

Fig. Bearish Harami

The word harami in Japanese means "Pregnant". A Bearish harami pattern consists of two candles, one mother and the other baby candle. It constitutes a small red candle that forms within the body of the previous larger green candle.

In this pattern, the length of the wicks is not very relevant. However, it is preferred that the wicks of the smaller red candle be inside the body of the larger green candle.

This pattern suggests that the buyers are losing control of the uptrend, and the sellers are starting to gain momentum in the market.

How to Trade a Bearish Harami Pattern?

After the formation of a bearish harami pattern, enter a short position when the price of the security starts trading below the opening price of the green candle. The stop-loss should be placed above the closing price of the green candle.

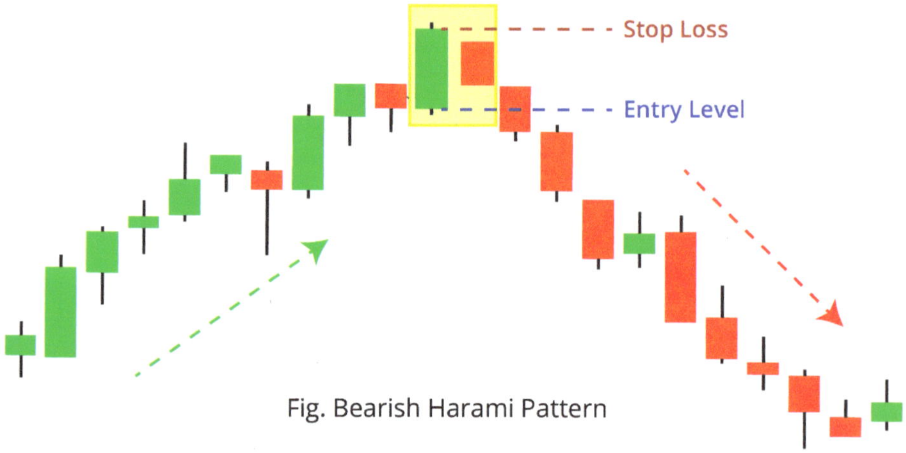

Fig. Bearish Harami Pattern

3) Bearish Harami Cross

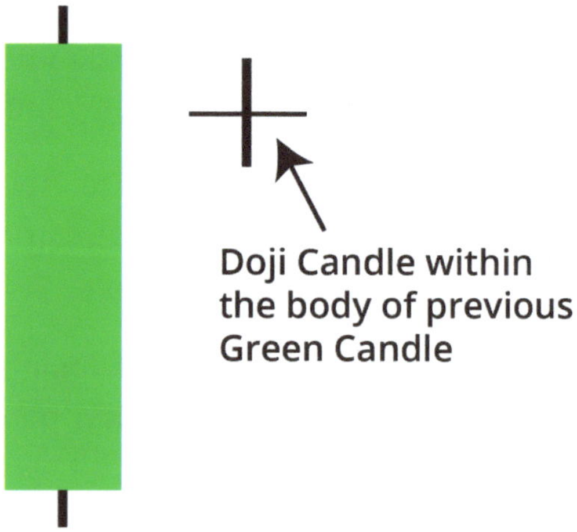

Fig. Bearish Harami Cross

A bearish harami cross is another reversal pattern that bears a resemblance to a bearish harami pattern. This pattern consists of a doji candle within the body of the previous green candle.

The occurrence of this pattern during an uptrend indicates the potential loss of momentum from buyers and sellers gaining control of the market. However, the strength of the sellers is only confirmed once the price of security starts trading below the opening price of the green candle.

How to Trade a Bearish Harami Cross Pattern?

The execution of a trade is similar to that of a bearish harami pattern. One can enter a short position when the price of the security starts trading below the opening price of the green candle, with the stop-loss placed at the closing price of the green candle.

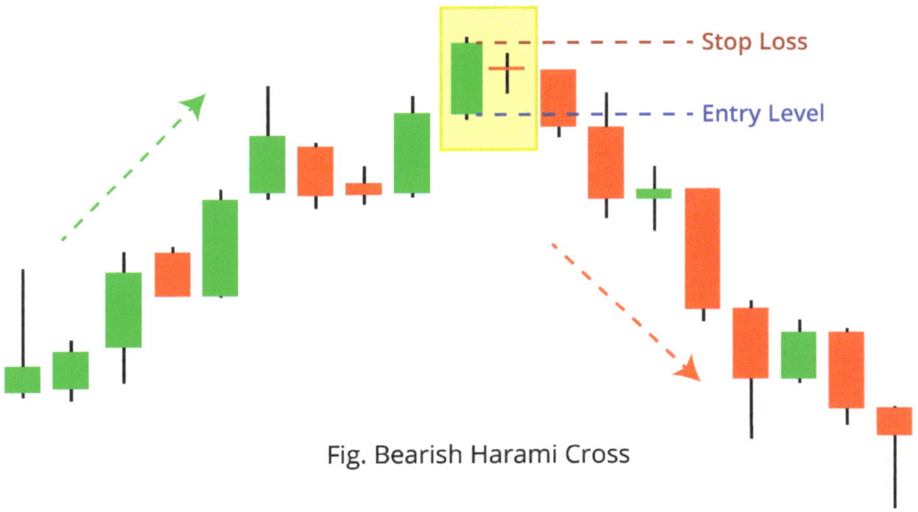

Fig. Bearish Harami Cross

4) Dark Cloud Cover

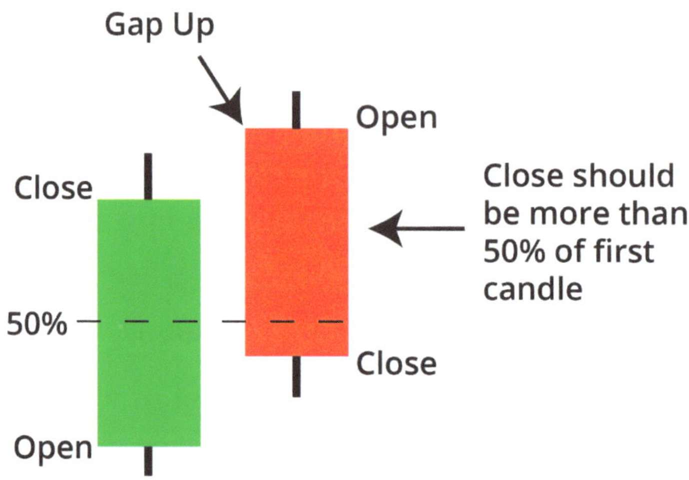

Fig. Dark Cloud Cover

The Dark cloud cover is a bearish reversal pattern consisting of a large green candle followed by a gap-up red candle. The red candle ends up closing below the mid-point of the previous green candle.

The red candle formation in this pattern during an uptrend suggests that although the buyers had a strong grip on the uptrend earlier, a strong inflow of sellers has entered, indicating a potential trend reversal.

How to Trade a Dark Cloud Cover?

One can enter in a short position using this pattern when the price of the security starts trading below the red candle. The stop-loss for this trade should be placed at the high of the candlestick pattern.

Fig. Dark cloud cover

5) Bearish Kicker Pattern

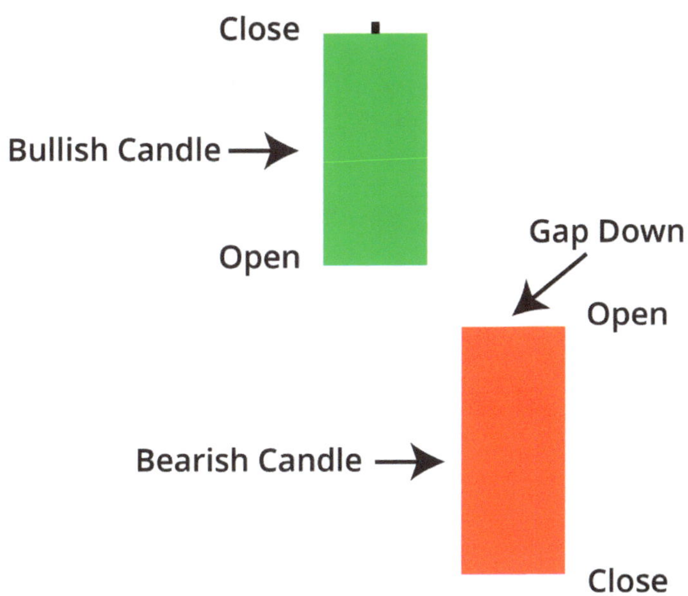

Fig. Bearish Kicker

The bearish kicker is a two-candlestick reversal pattern that constitutes a green candle followed by a gap-down red candle. Here, the red candle should open below the body of the green candle.

The first green candle in the pattern suggests that the buyers were earlier in control of the security. However, the sudden appearance of the red candle indicates that the sellers have aggressively entered and pushed the prices lower.

How to Trade a Bearish Kicker Pattern?

One can enter a short position in the security when the price starts trading below the low of the kicker pattern. The stop-loss for this trade is at the opening price of the green candle.

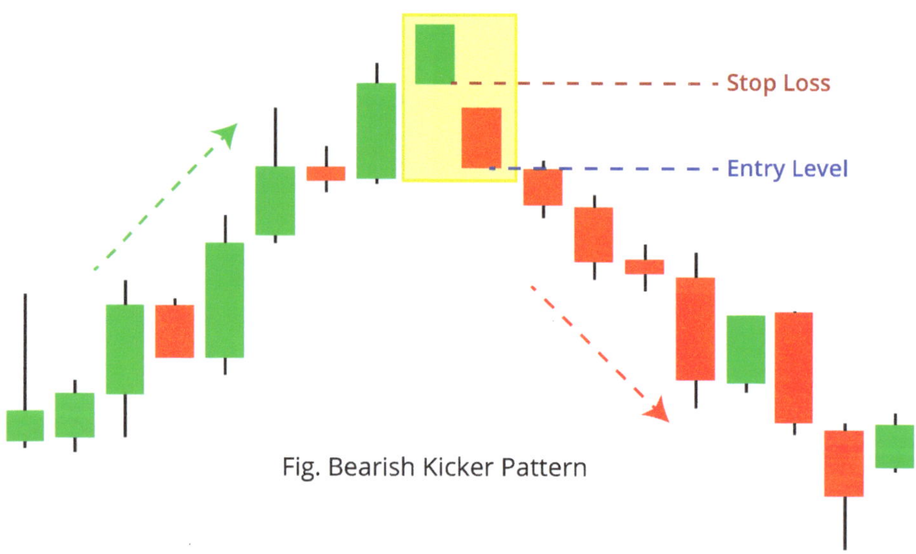

Fig. Bearish Kicker Pattern

6) Tweezer Top

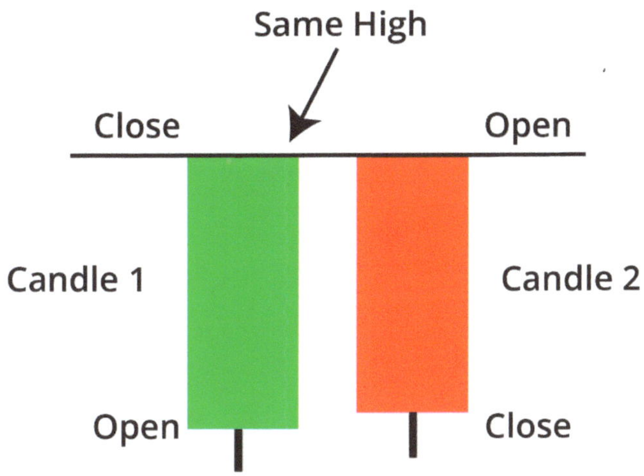

Fig. Tweezer Top

The Tweezer top is a bearish reversal pattern that consists of two candlesticks with the same highs. The first candle should be a green candle that is part of the existing uptrend, and the second candle should preferably be a red candle that has the same high as the preceding green candle.

This pattern suggests that the buyers have been exhausted and the sellers have entered the security. It is more suited if the pattern appears near a significant resistance level.

How to Trade a Tweezer Top Pattern?

One can enter a short position in the security when the price starts trading below the low of the red candle. The stop-loss for this trade should be at the high of the pattern.

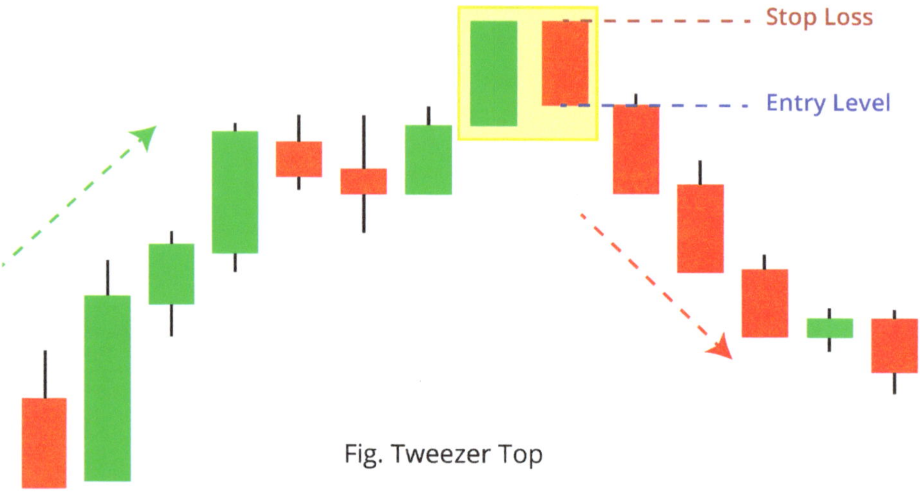

Fig. Tweezer Top

7) Bearish Counterattack

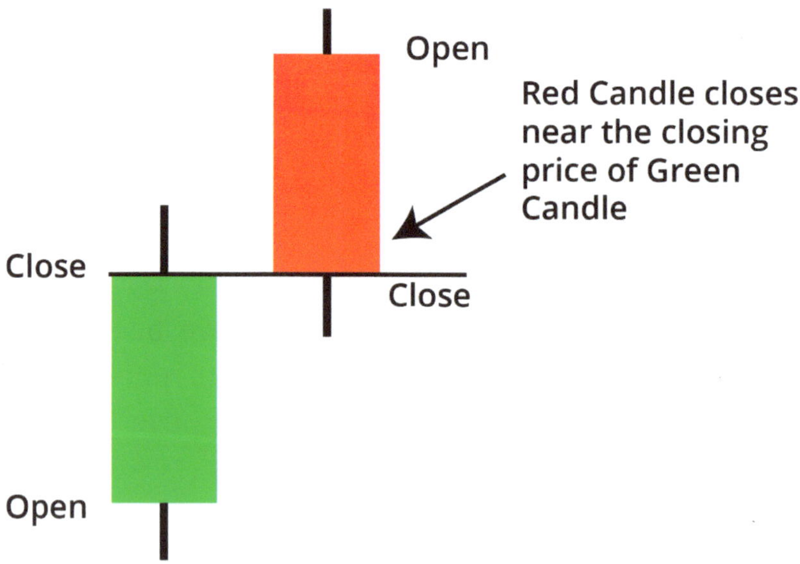

Fig. Bearish Counterattack

The bearish counterattack is a reversal pattern that constitutes a green candle followed by a gap-up red candle that closes near the closing price of the green candle.

This pattern indicates that the buyers were earlier in control of the price of security. However, the sudden entrance of the sellers suggests that the buying pressure is weakening in the security.

How to Trade a Bearish Counterattack Pattern?

One can enter a short position in the security when the price starts trading below the low of the red candle of this pattern. Simultaneously, place a stop-loss above the high of the red candle.

Fig. Bearish Counterattack

8) Bearish Thrusting Pattern

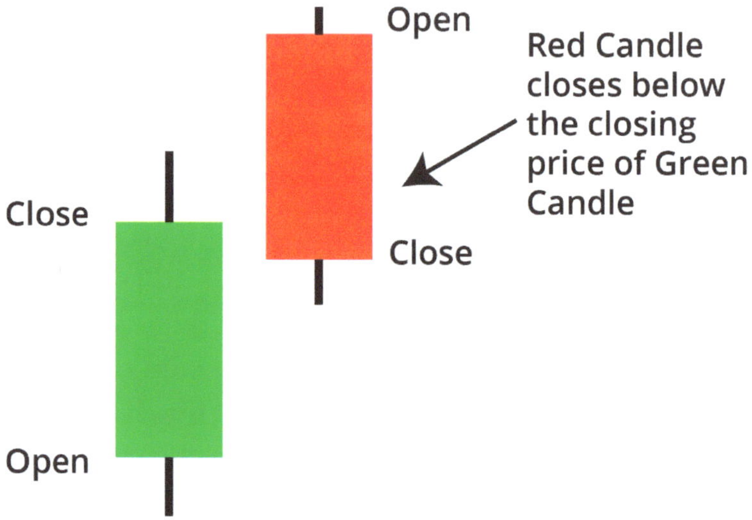

Fig. Bearish Thrusting Pattern

This pattern looks similar to that of a bearish counterattack pattern. It comprises a green candle followed by a gap-up red candle. But the Bearish Thrusting Pattern differs from the bearish counterattack as the red candle closes below the closing price of the green candle and above the midpoint of the green candle.

This pattern suggests that sellers are intervening in the buying pressure and trying to push the price down. This pattern can indicate both a potential bullish continuation as well as a potential bearish reversal based on the overall context of the market.

How to Trade a Bearish Thrusting Pattern?

As this pattern suggests a move in either direction, there are two ways one can enter a trade.

If the security is trading below the red candle, enter a short position in the security and simultaneously place a stop-loss above the high of the red candle.

Fig. Bearish Thrusting pattern

If the price of the security starts trading above the red candle, one can enter a long position and simultaneously place a stop-loss below the low of the red candle.

9) Falling Window

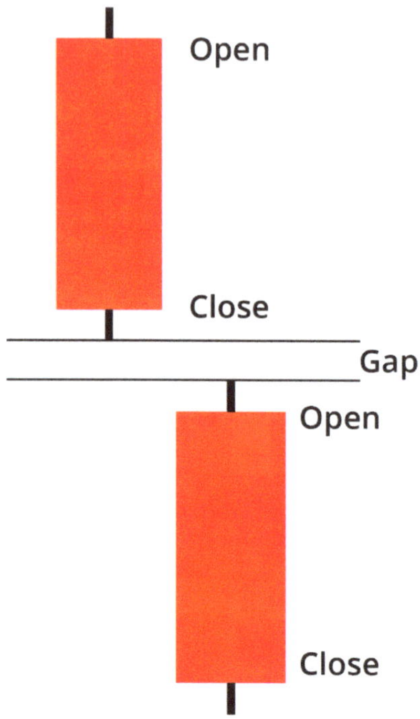

Fig. Falling Window

A falling window is a bearish continuation pattern that comprises two consecutive red candles. Here, the low and high of the first and second red candles are separated by a gap opening between them. This pattern suggests a strong bearish sentiment in the security.

How to Trade a Falling Window Pattern?

After the formation of the pattern, enter a short position in the security if the price starts trading below the low of the second red candle. Here, the Gap will work as a resistance. The stop-loss for this trade should be placed at the low of the first red candle.

Fig. Falling Window

10) Bearish Homing Pigeon

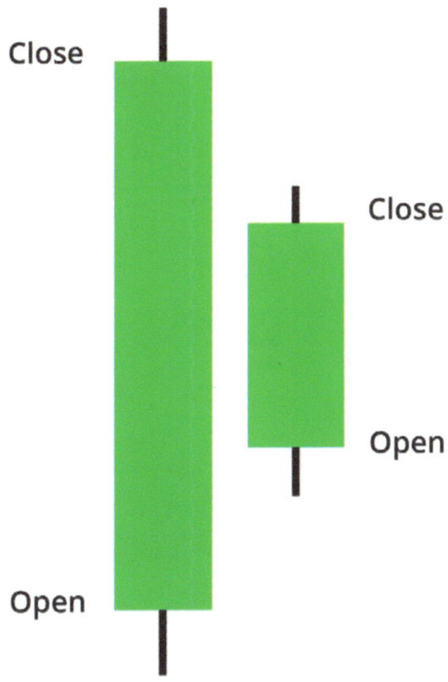

Fig. Bearish Homing Pigeon

The bearish homing pigeon is a reversal pattern that consists of two green candles, where the first candle is a large green candle and the second candle is a smaller green candle that fits within the body of the first candle.

The appearance of this pattern near a resistance level suggests that the buyers are losing the momentum of the security.

How to Trade a Bearish Homing Pigeon Pattern?

One can enter a short position using this bearish homing pigeon pattern when the price of the security starts trading below the low of the second candle. However, a risk-averse trader can also wait for the price of the security to cross below the low of the first candle to enter the trade.

The stop-loss for this trade should be placed above the first candle of the Homing Pigeon pattern.

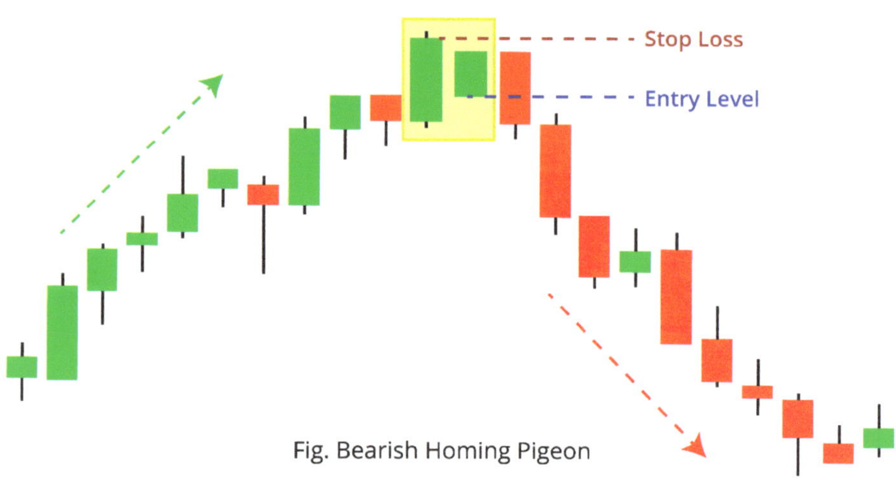

Fig. Bearish Homing Pigeon

11) Bearish On Neck Pattern

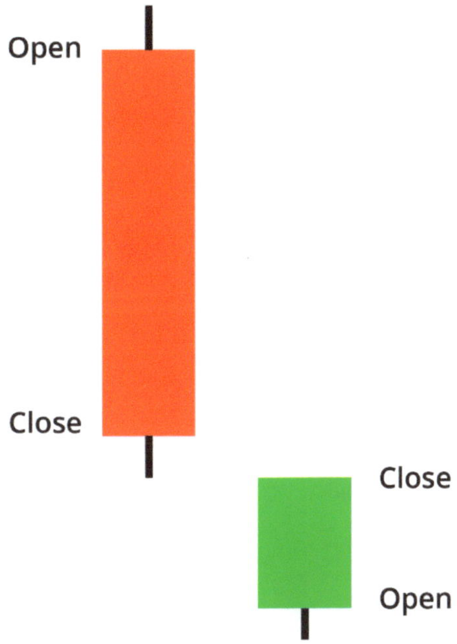

Fig. Bearish On Neck Pattern

The Bearish On Neck pattern is a continuation pattern that occurs when a large red candle is followed by a gap-down green candle that closes at the same or below the closing price of the prior red candle. The second candle can be in any shape but should have a smaller body than the prior red candle.

This pattern indicates that the buyers failed to overpower the sellers in the security, and the bearish trend will likely continue further.

How to Trade a Bearish in Neck Pattern?

One can enter a short position in the security when the price starts trading below the low of the green candle of the pattern.

Simultaneously, one should place the stop-loss above the high of the first red candle.

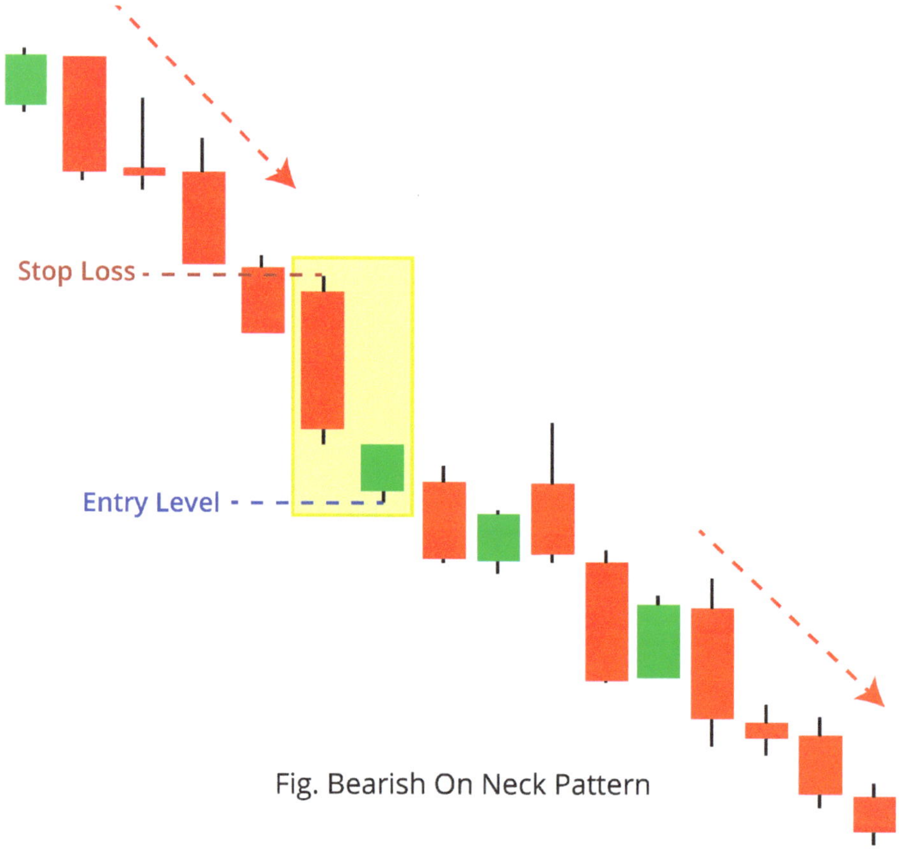

Fig. Bearish On Neck Pattern

BULLISH TRIPLE CANDLESTICK PATTERN

The Bullish Triple Candlestick Pattern consists of candle patterns that inherently represent bullishness by nature and consist of three consecutive candlesticks. Here, you need to look into all three candles, i.e. the first, second and third candle, to get the confirmation of the pattern.

1) Three White Soldiers

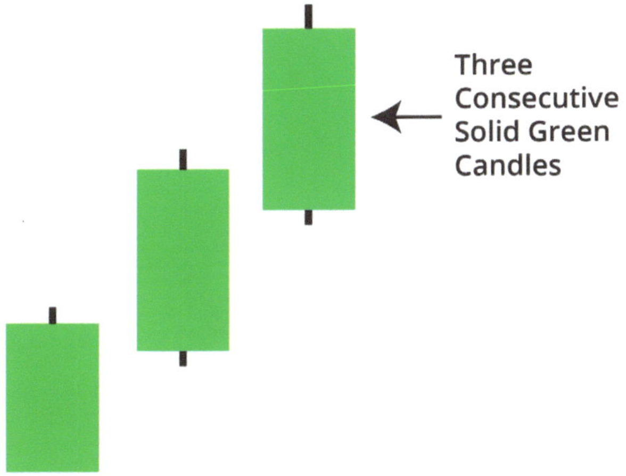

Fig. Three White Soldier

The three white soldiers is a bullish reversal pattern that is formed at the bottom of the downtrend. This candlestick pattern comprises three large green candles and each closes higher than the prior candle. These candles should preferably have small or no upper wicks and short lower wicks, indicating that buyers are in control of the security.

The formation of this pattern indicates that the bearish sentiment has ended, and the momentum of the buyers is increasing in the security. The best-case scenario for this pattern to appear is near a support level.

How to trade the Three White Soldiers Pattern?

After the formation of the Three White Soldiers pattern, one can enter a long position when the price of the security starts trading above the high of the third candle of the pattern. Simultaneously, one can place a stop-loss at the low of the first candle.

Fig. Three White Soldiers

2) Morning Star

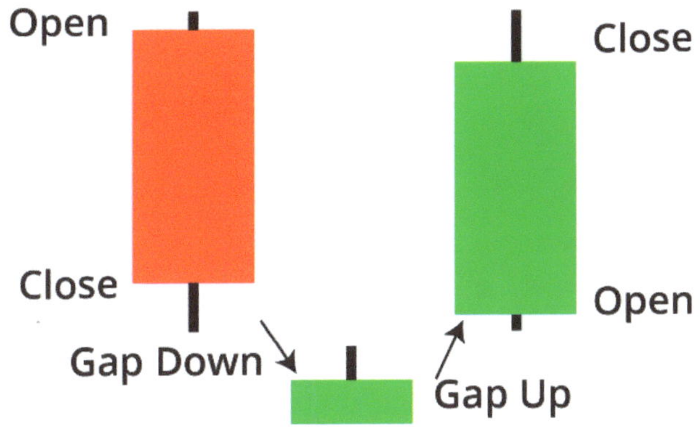

Fig. Morning Star

The Morning Star is a bullish reversal pattern that is formed at the bottom of a downtrend. This pattern comprises the following candles:

1. A large red candle, which is a part of the downtrend
2. A small-bodied candle (green or red) that opens gap-down.
3. A large green candle that opens gap-up and closes above the midpoint of the first red candle.

This pattern indicates the momentum of the sellers has ended, and the buyers have gained momentum in the security.

How to Trade a Morning Star Pattern?

One can look to enter a long position in the security when the price starts trading above the third candle. Simultaneously, a stop-loss should be placed below the low of the second candle.

Fig. Morning Star

3) Morning Doji Star

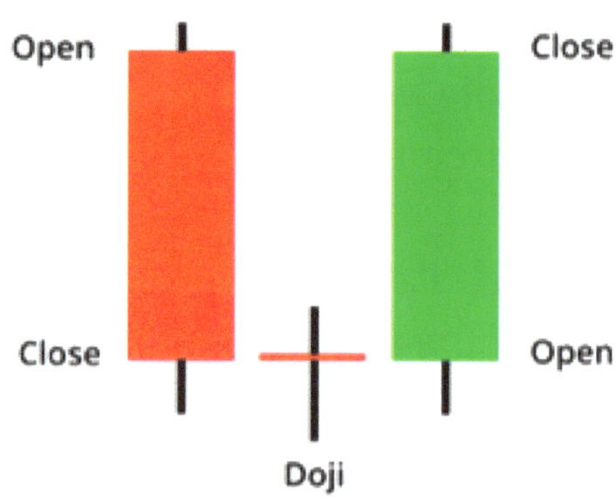

Fig. Morning Doji Star

The Morning Doji Star is a bullish reversal pattern and has similar characteristics to the Morning Star Pattern. This pattern comprises of the following candles:

1. A large red candle, which is a part of the downtrend
2. A Doji candle that is formed near or below the close of the prior red candle
3. A large green candle that opens near the close of previous doji pattern and closes above the midpoint of the first red candle.

This pattern indicates indecision between the buyers and sellers, followed by the buyers gaining momentum in the security.

How to Trade a Morning Doji Star Pattern?

One can look to enter a long position in the security when the price starts above the third candle. Simultaneously, a stop-loss should be placed at the low of the doji candle formed in the pattern.

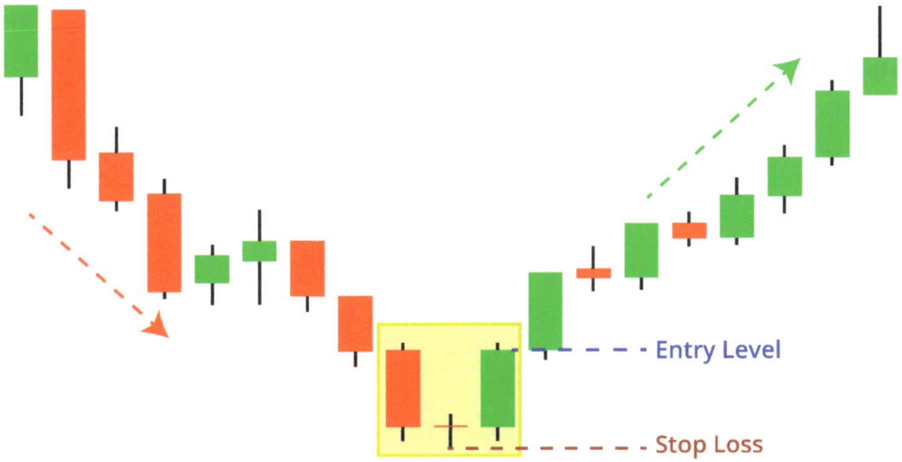

Fig. Morning Doji Star

4) Bullish Abandoned Baby Pattern

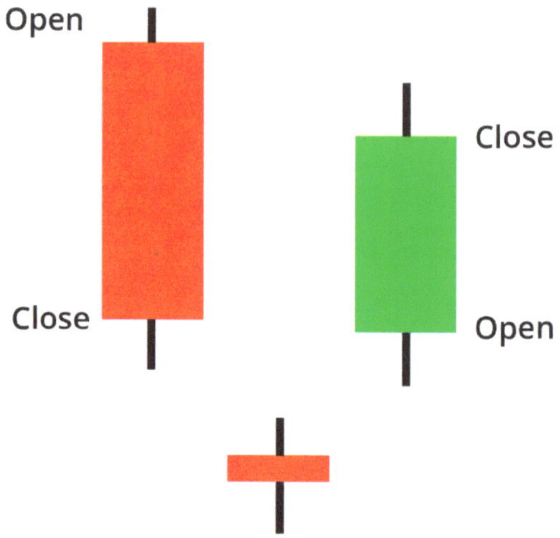

Fig. Bullish Abandoned Baby

The Bullish Abandoned Baby Pattern is a rare yet strong candlestick pattern that signals a reversal in the market. This pattern has similar candlestick constituents to the Morning Doji star pattern. However, the doji candle in this pattern is completely separated from the other two candles. Hence the name 'Abandoned Baby'.

This is a bullish reversal pattern and suggests that the buyers have overpowered the sellers, which has led to the change of sentiment from bearish to bullish.

How to Trade a Bullish Abandoned Baby Pattern?

One can look to enter a long position in the security when the price starts trading above the closing price of the third candle (or above the entire pattern for risk averse traders). Simultaneously, a stop-loss should be placed below the low of the doji candle.

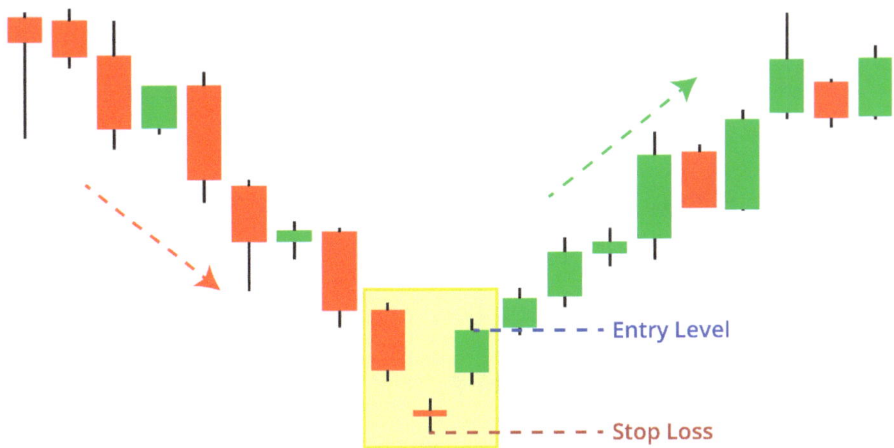

Fig. Bullish Abandoned Baby Pattern

5) Three Inside Up

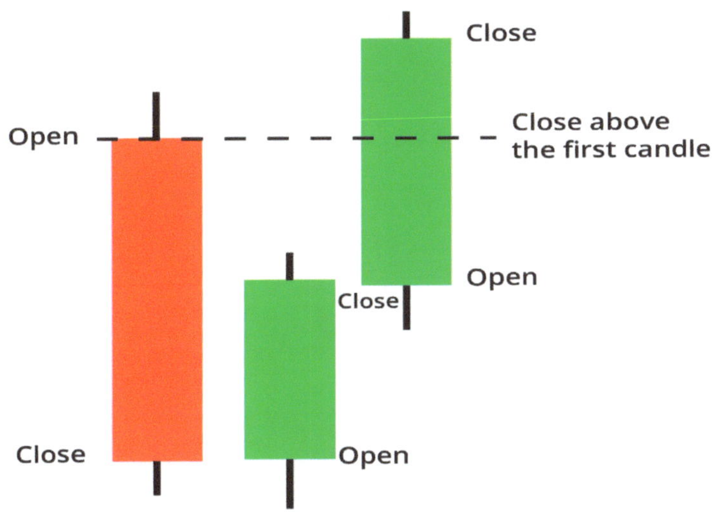

Fig. Three Inside Up

The three inside up is a bullish reversal candlestick pattern found at the bottom of the downtrend. This pattern comprises the following three candles:

1. A large red candle that is a part of the previous downtrend
2. A second green candle within the first red candle
3. A large green candle that closes above the large red candle that signals a bullish reversal

This pattern suggests that the selling pressure is weakening and buyers are taking control of the security

How to Trade a Three Inside Up Pattern?

One can look to enter a long position in the security when the price starts above the third candle. Simultaneously, a stop-loss should be placed below the low of the pattern.

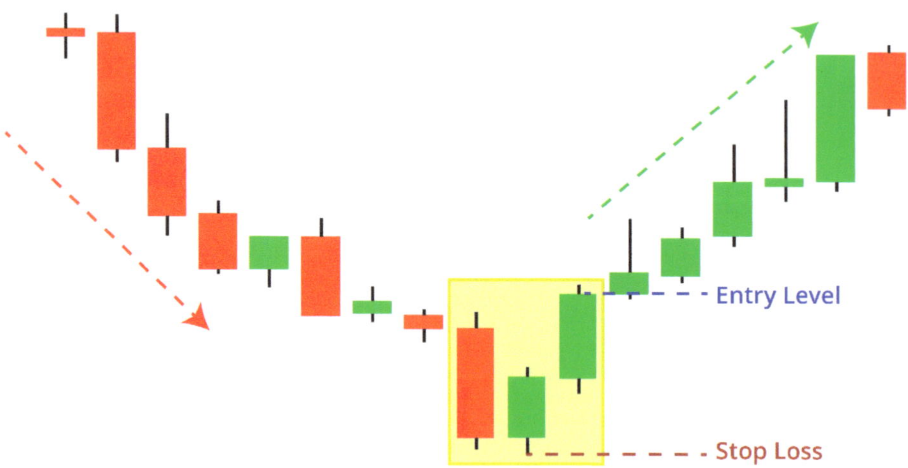

Fig. Three Inside Up

6) Three Outside Up

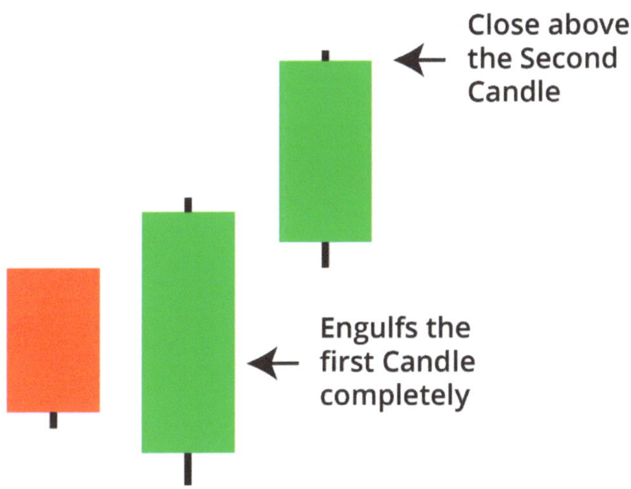

Fig. Three outside Up

The three outside up is a reversal candlestick pattern found at the bottom of the downtrend. This pattern comprises the following candles:

1. A red candle, which is a part of the downtrend.
2. A large green candle that engulfs the prior red candle.
3. Another green candle that closes above the second green candle.

This pattern suggests that the selling pressure is weakening, and buyers are taking control of the security.

How to Trade a Three Outside Up Pattern?

One can look to enter a long position in the security when the price starts above the third candle. Simultaneously, a stop-loss should be placed below the low of the candle pattern.

Fig. Three Outside Up

7) Upside Tasuki Gap

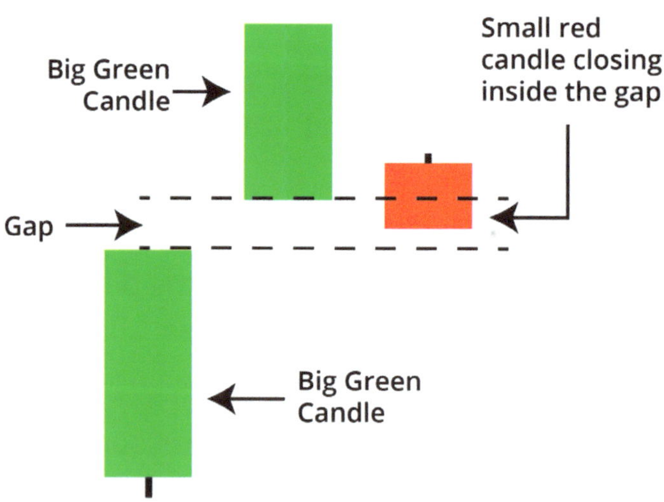

Fig. Upside Tasuki Gap

The Upside Tasuki Gap is a continuation pattern that can appear in the middle of an uptrend. This pattern comprises the following three candles:

1. A large green candle that is a part of the existing uptrend.
2. Another green candle that opens the gap up above the first candle
3. The third candle is a red candle that closes between the gap created by the prior two green candles.

This pattern suggests that the sellers entered the security during a bullish trend but failed to push the price lower. This suggests that the bullish trend is likely going to continue.

How to Trade an Upside Tasuki Gap?

One can look to enter a long position in the security when the price starts above the red candle. Simultaneously, a stop-loss should be placed below the closing of the first green candle.

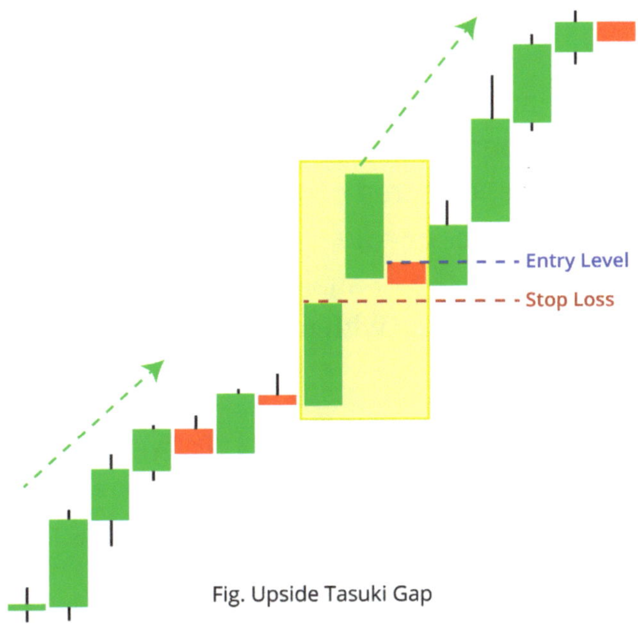

Fig. Upside Tasuki Gap

8) Three Stars in the South

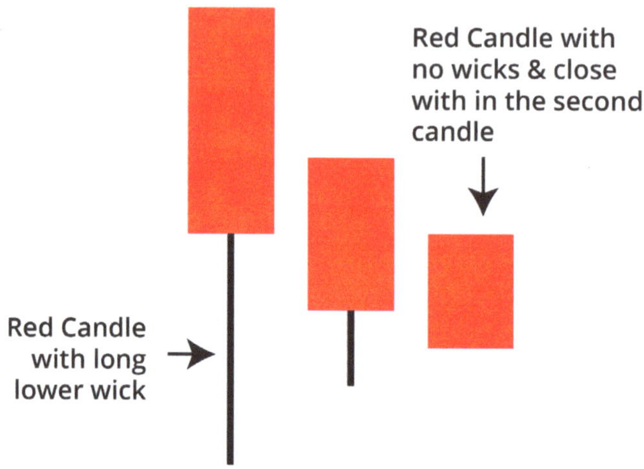

Fig. Three Stars In The South

The three stars in the South is a rare bullish candlestick pattern that indicates a reversal in the market. This pattern comprises the following three candles:

1. First, a large-bodied red candle with a long lower wick and no upper wick.
2. Second, a shorter red candle with a lower wick above the low of the prior candle
3. The Third candle is again a smaller red candle with no wicks and a close within the high and low range of the second candle.

The appearance of this pattern is rare, and it indicates a weakening strength of the sellers. However, the pattern does not necessarily indicate an upward movement. Rather it signifies an end of the existing downward trend.

How to Trade a Three-Stars South Pattern?

When the price of the security goes up and crosses above the third candle, it is a confirmation to enter a long position in the trade. A stop-loss should be placed below the low of the first candle.

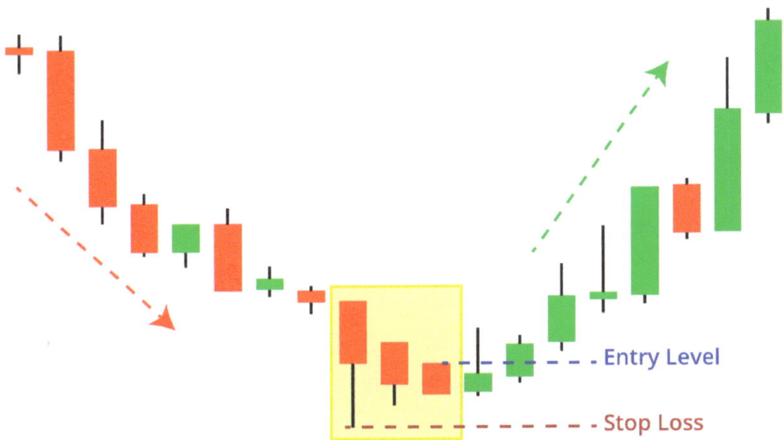

Fig. Three Stars in the South

9) Up Gap Side-By-Side White Lines

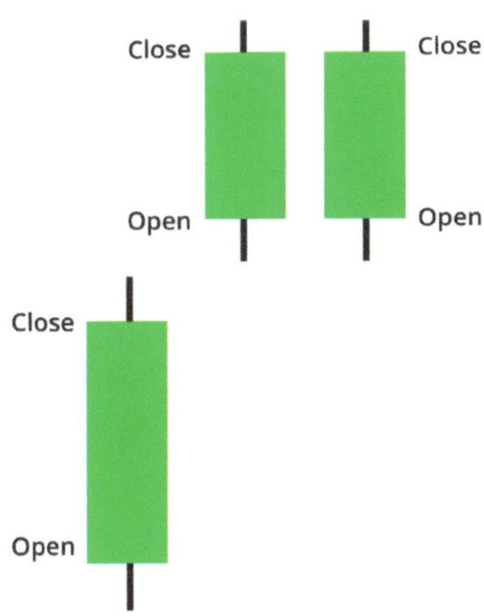

Fig. Up Gap Side By Side White Lines

The Up Gap Side-by-Side white lines pattern is a bullish continuation pattern that can appear in the middle of an existing uptrend. This pattern comprises the following candles:

1. A large green candle that is a part of the existing uptrend.
2. The second candle opens at a Gap-up above the close of the first candle, followed by the third candle of similar size and trading in the similar range as the second candle.

This pattern suggests that the buyers anticipate further upward movement in the price and continue buying the security.

How to trade an Up Gap Side By Side Pattern?

One can look to enter a long position in the security when the price starts trading above the third candle. Simultaneously, a stop-loss should be placed below the low of the second or the third green candle.

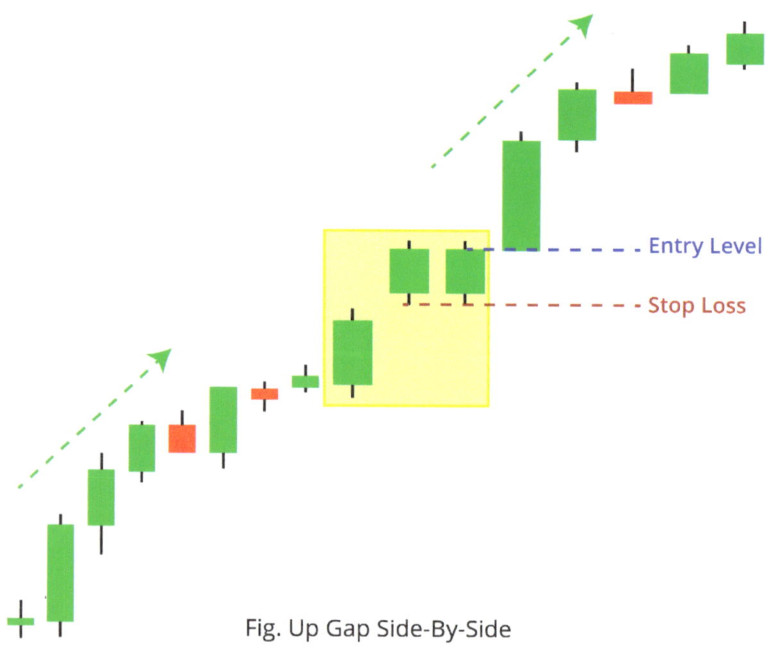

Fig. Up Gap Side-By-Side

10) Bullish Tri Star

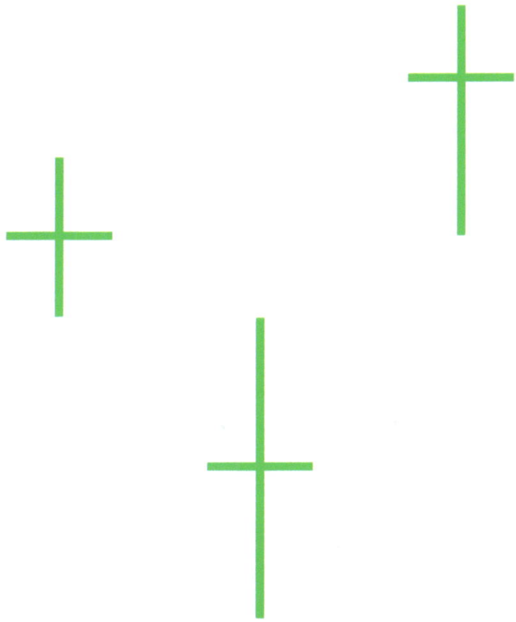

Fig. Bullish Tri Star

The Bullish tri star is a rare candlestick pattern that can indicate a reversal after a downtrend. This candlestick pattern comprises of three consecutive doji patterns. Here, the second doji forms after a gap down, and the third doji appears after a gap up.

How to Trade a Bullish Tri Star?

One can look to enter a long position in the security when the price starts trading above the third Doji candle. Simultaneously, one can place a stop loss at the low of the second doji pattern.

Fig. Bullish Tri Star

11) Bullish Stick Sandwich

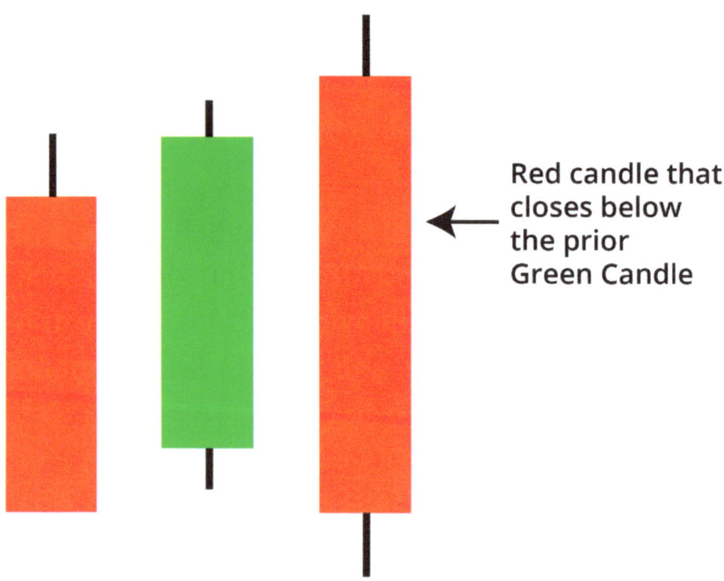

Fig. Bullish Stick Sandwich

This candlestick pattern resembles the shape of a sandwich on the trader's screen. The Bullish Stick Sandwich is a candlestick pattern that suggests a bullish reversal after a downtrend. This pattern comprises the following three candles:

1. A large red candle that is a part of the downtrend
2. A small green candle
3. Another red candle that closes below the prior green candle.

The appearance of the green candlestick in this pattern indicates the entrance of the buyers in the security, suggesting a potential bullish trend reversal.

How to Trade a Bullish Stick Sandwich?

To trade this candlestick pattern, wait for another green candle to close above the third candle to confirm the entry. One can enter a long position in the security when the price starts trading above the confirmation candle. The stop-loss for this trade should be kept at the low of the candlestick pattern.

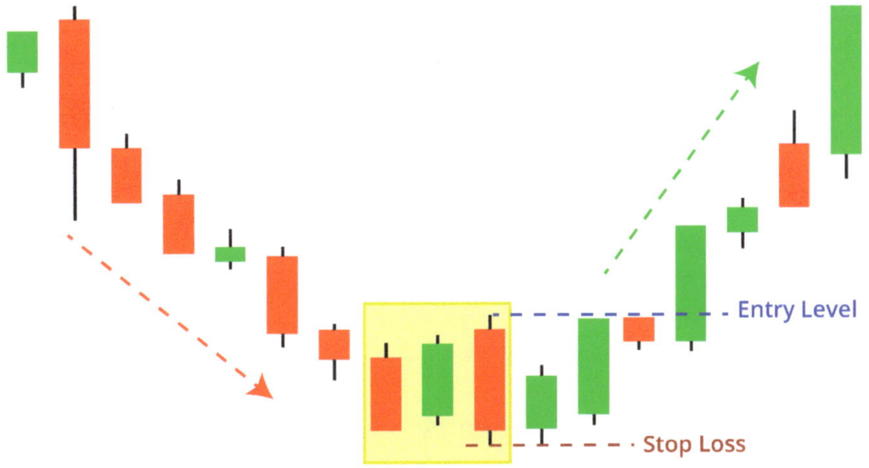

Fig. Bullish Stick Sandwich

BEARISH TRIPLE CANDLESTICK PATTERN

In this chapter, we'll discuss the Bearish Triple Candlestick Patterns. Similar to the Bullish Triple Candlestick Patterns, these candlesticks consist of three consecutive candle patterns but are inherently bearish by nature. Here again, you need to look into all three consecutive candles to get the confirmation of the trade.

1) Three Black Crows

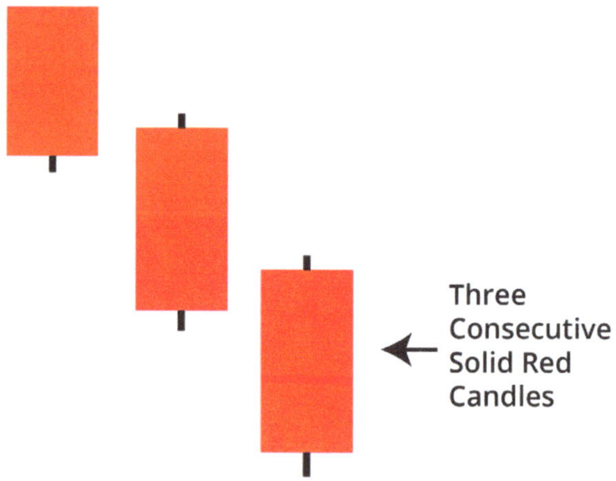

Fig. Three Black Crows

The three black crows is a bearish reversal pattern that is formed at the top of an uptrend. This candlestick pattern comprises three large red candles, each having a close lower than the prior candle. These candles should preferably have no or very short lower and upper wicks, indicating that sellers are in control of the security.

The formation of this pattern indicates that the bullish sentiment has ended and the momentum of the sellers is increasing in the security. The best-case scenario for this pattern to appear is near a resistance level.

How to Trade The Three Black Crows Pattern?

After the formation of the Three Black Crows pattern, enter a short position when the price of the security starts trading below the low of the third candle of the pattern. Simultaneously, place a stop-loss above the high of the first candle of this pattern to avoid premature stopping out.

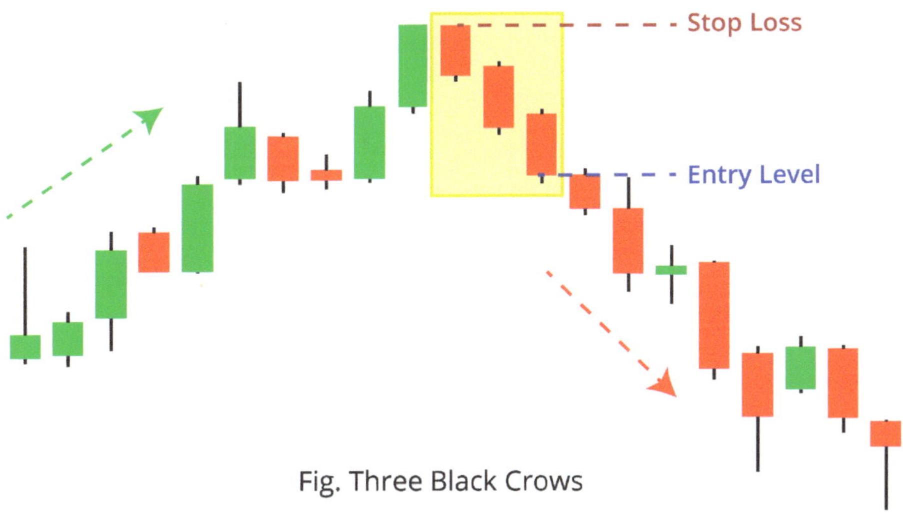

Fig. Three Black Crows

2) Evening Star

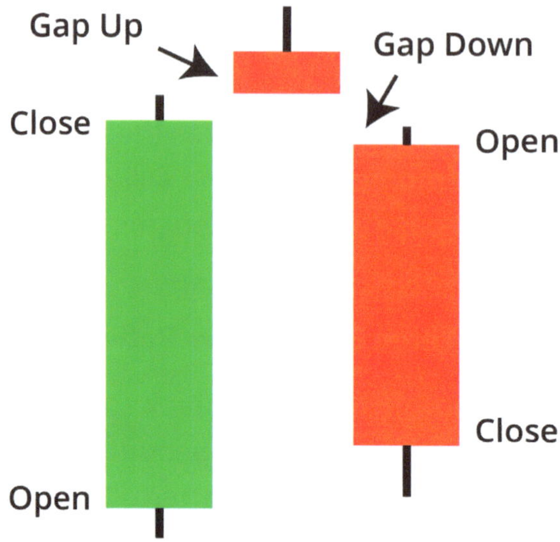

Fig. Evening Star

The Evening Star is another powerful bearish reversal pattern that is formed at the top of an uptrend. This pattern is comprised of the following three candles:

1. A large green candle, which is a part of the uptrend.
2. A small-bodied candle (green or red) that opens at a gap-up to the previous candle.
3. A large red candle that opens gap-down and closes below the midpoint of the first green candle.

This pattern indicates that the momentum of the buyers has ended, and the sellers have gained power in the security.

How to Trade an Evening Star Pattern?

While trading with the Evening Star pattern, one can look to enter a short position in the security when the price starts trading below the third red candle. Simultaneously, a stop-loss should be placed above the high of the second candle.

Fig. Evening Star

3) Evening Doji Star

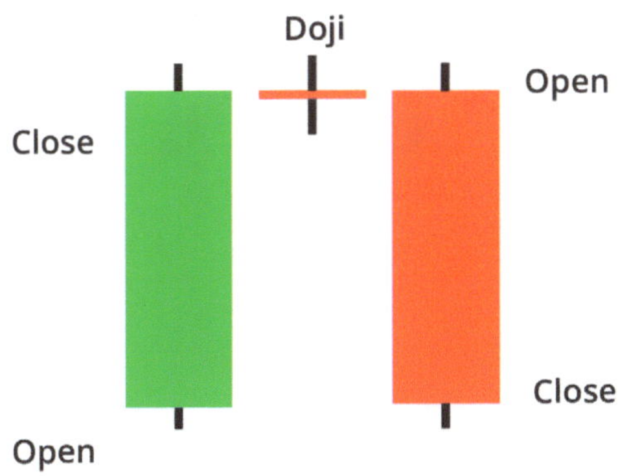

Fig. Evening Doji Star

The Evening Doji Star is a bearish reversal pattern and has characteristics similar to the Evening Star Pattern. This pattern comprises the following three candles:

1. A large green candle, which is a part of the uptrend
2. A Doji second candle which is formed near or above the close of the green candle
3. The third candle is a large red candle that opens near the close of the doji candle and closes below the midpoint of the first green candle.

The Doji pattern in the middle indicates indecision between the buyers and sellers, followed by the sellers gaining momentum in the security.

How to trade an Evening Doji Star Pattern?

One can look to enter a short position in the security when the price starts trading below the third candle. Simultaneously, a stop-loss should be placed above the high of the doji candle.

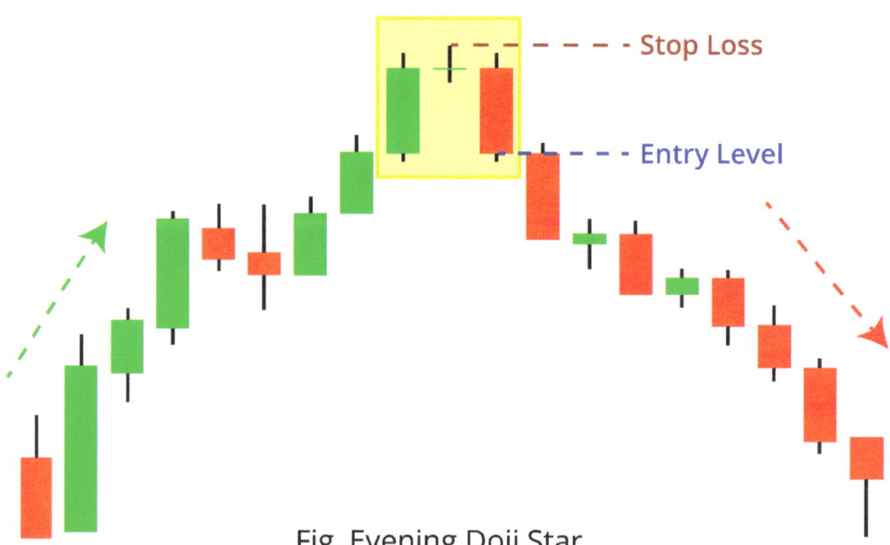

Fig. Evening Doji Star

4) Bearish Abandoned Baby Pattern

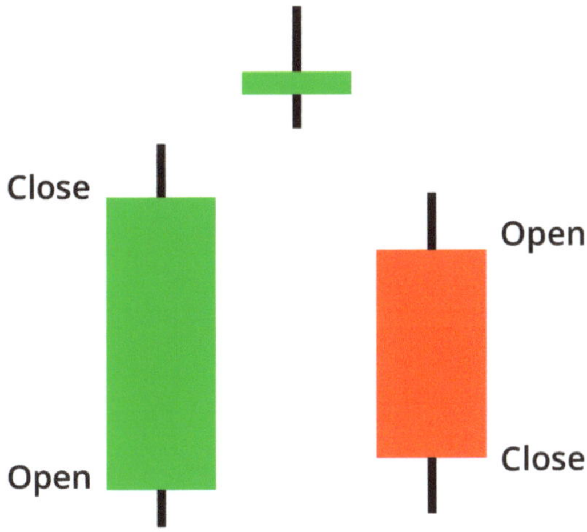

Fig. Bearish Abandoned Baby

The Bearish Abandoned Baby Pattern is another rare yet strong candlestick pattern that signals a bearish reversal in the market. This pattern has similar candlestick constituents to the Evening Doji star pattern. However, the doji candle in this pattern is completely separated from the other two candles, hence suggesting an abandoned baby.

This pattern suggests that the sellers have overpowered the buyers, which has led to the change of sentiment from bullish to bearish.

How to trade a Bearish Abandoned Baby Pattern?

One can look to enter a short position in the security when the price starts trading below the third candle. Simultaneously, a stop-loss should be placed above the high of the doji candle.

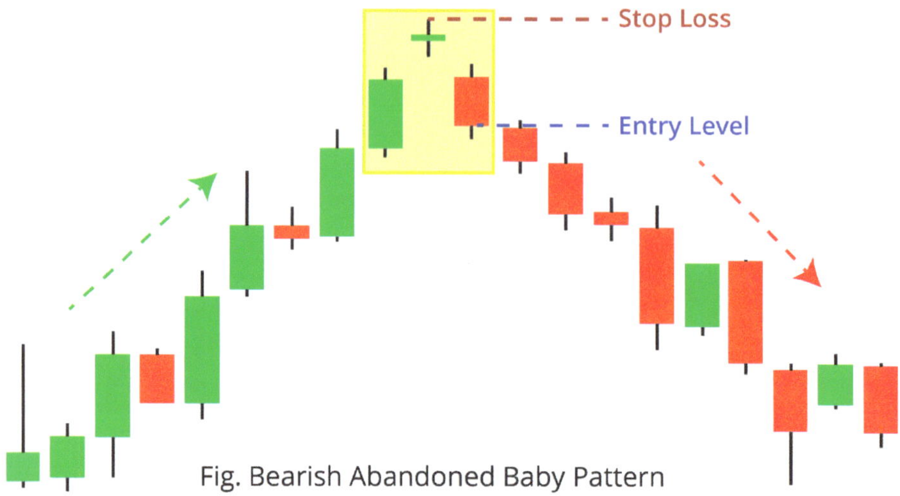

Fig. Bearish Abandoned Baby Pattern

5) Three Inside Down

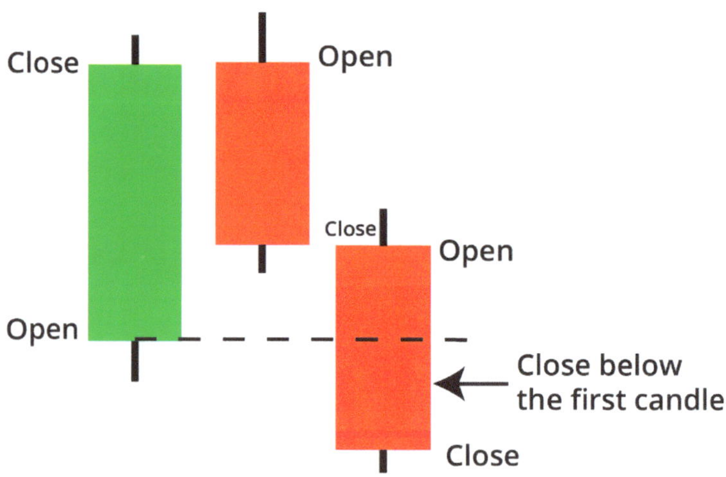

Fig. Three Inside Down

The three inside down is a bearish reversal candlestick pattern found at the top of the uptrend. This pattern comprises the following three candles:

1. A large green candle that is a part of the previous uptrend
2. The Second candle is a small red candle that closes within the body of the first green candle
3. Third is a large red candle that closes below the first green candle.

This pattern suggests that the buying pressure has weakened, and sellers are now taking control of the security.

How to trade a Three Inside Down Pattern?

One can look to enter a short position in the security when the price starts trading below the third candle. Simultaneously, a stop-loss should be placed above the high of the entire pattern.

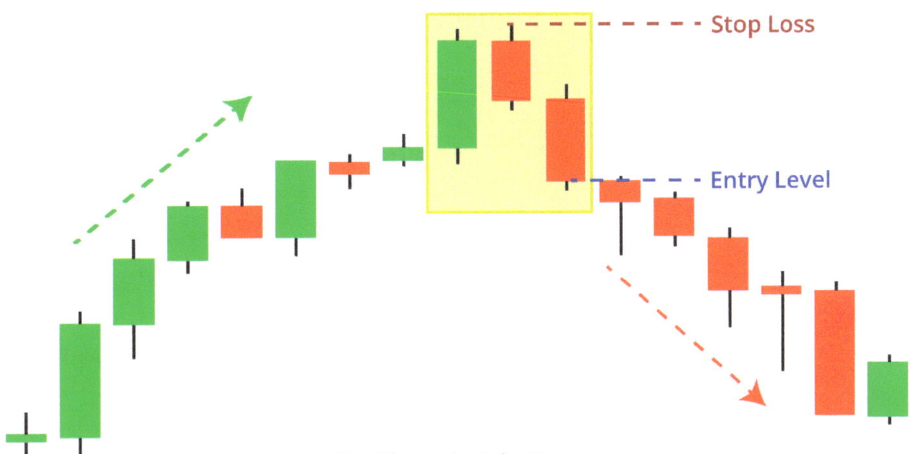

Fig. Three Inside Down

6) Three Outside Down

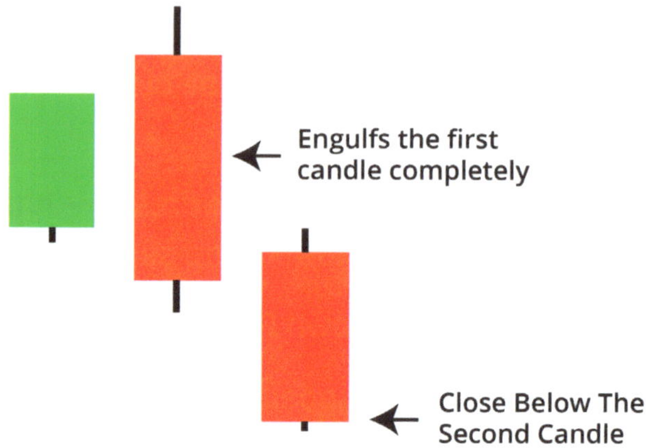

Fig. Three Outside Down

The three outside down is another bearish reversal candlestick pattern found at the top of the uptrend. This pattern comprises the following three candles:

1. A green candle, which is a part of the existing uptrend.
2. A large red candle that engulfs the prior green candle.
3. The third red candle closes below the second red candle.

This pattern suggests that the sellers have taken charge of the security, and a bearish downtrend may appear.

How to trade a Three Outside Down Pattern?

One can look to enter a short position in the security when the price starts trading below the third candle. Simultaneously, a stop-loss should be placed above the high of the entire candle pattern to avoid premature stopping out.

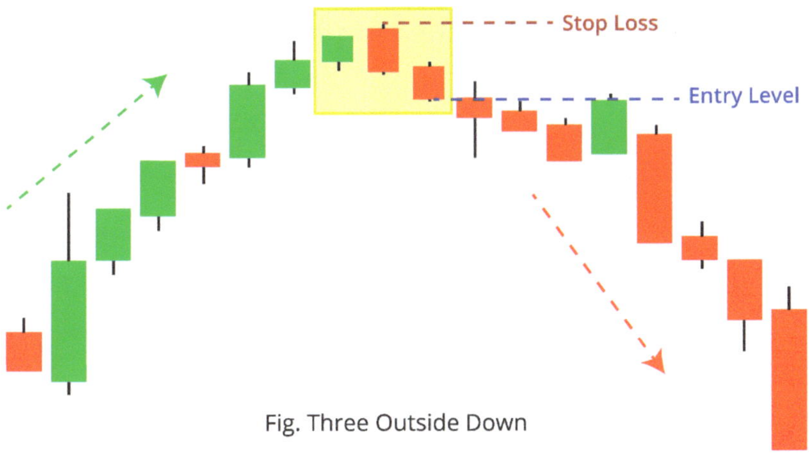

Fig. Three Outside Down

7) Downside Tasuki Gap

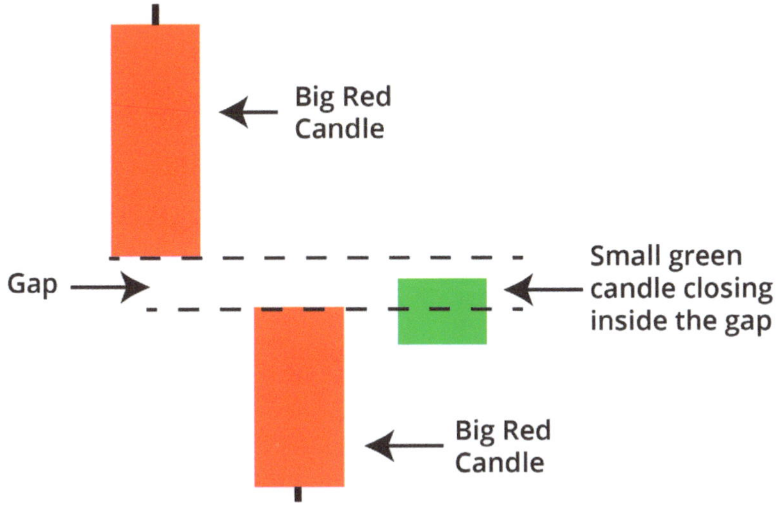

Fig. Downside Tasuki Gap

The Downside Tasuki Gap is a downward continuation that can appear in the middle of a downtrend. This pattern comprises the following three candles:

1. A large red candle that is a part of the existing downtrend.
2. Another red candle opens at a gap down below the first candle
3. The third candle is a green candle that closes between the gap created by the two prior red candles.

This pattern suggests that the buyers entered the security during a bearish trend but failed to push the price higher. This suggests that the bearish trend is likely to continue.

How to trade a Downside Tasuki Gap?

One can look to enter a short position in the security when the price starts trading below the third green candle, as it confirms that the downtrend will continue. Simultaneously, a stop-loss should be placed above the low of the first red candle.

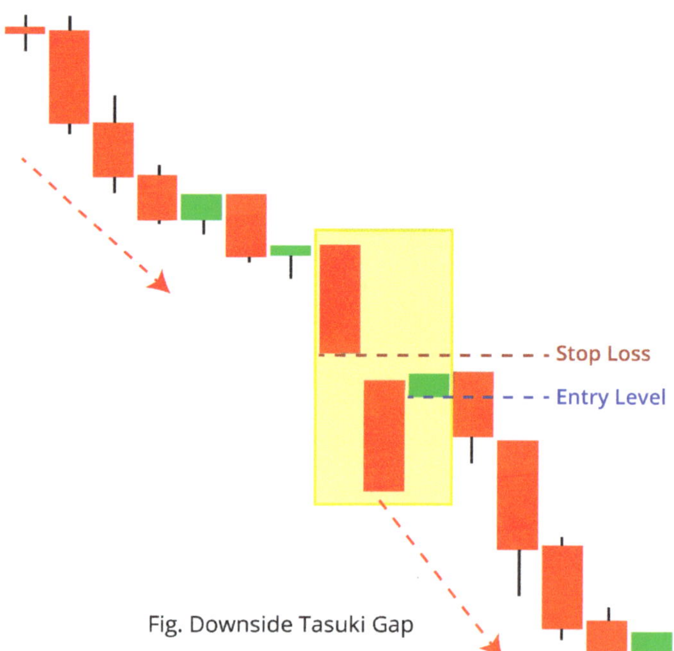

Fig. Downside Tasuki Gap

8) Three Stars in the North

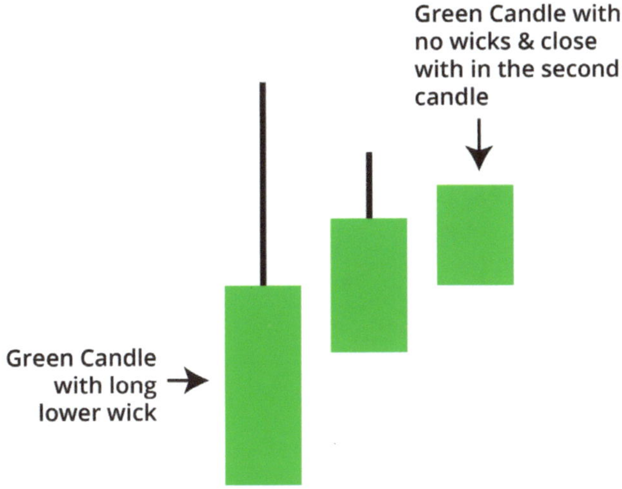

Fig. Three Stars In The North

The Three Stars in the North is a rare bearish candlestick pattern that indicates a reversal in the market. Although it consists of three green candles, the combination of these consecutive candle patterns suggests that the bullish trend may end. This pattern comprises the following three candles:

1. The large green candle has a long upper wick and no lower wick.
2. A shorter green candle with an upper wick below the high of the prior candle
3. An even smaller green candle with no wicks.

The appearance of this pattern indicates a weakening strength of the buyers. However, the pattern does not necessarily indicate a downward movement. Rather, it signifies an end of the existing upward trend.

How to trade a Three-Stars in the North Pattern?

When the price of the security crosses below the third candle, it is a confirmation to enter a short position in the trade. Here, the stop-loss should be placed above the high of the first candle to avoid premature stopping out.

Fig. Three Stars in the North

9) Down Gap Side By Side

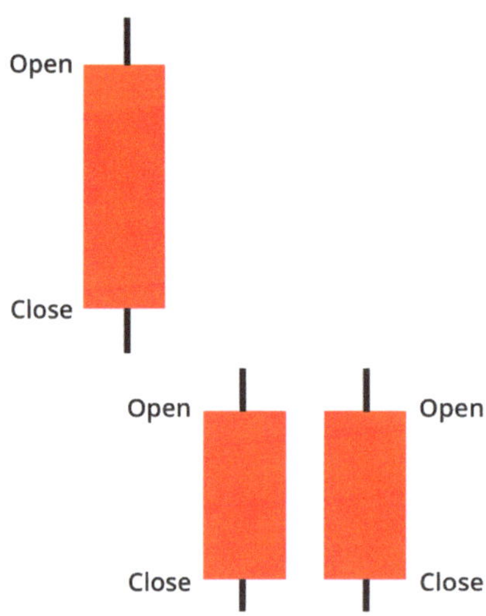

Fig. Down Gap Side By Side

The Down Gap Side-By-Side pattern is another downward continuation pattern that can appear in the middle of an existing downtrend. This pattern comprises the following candles:

1. A large red candle that is a part of the existing downtrend.
2. A gap-down followed by two red candles that are similar in size and trading in a similar range.

This pattern suggests that the sellers anticipate further downward movement in the price, and the selling may continue in the security.

How to trade a Down Gap Side By Side Pattern?

One can look to enter a short position in the security when the price starts trading below the third red candle. Simultaneously, a stop-loss should be placed above the highs of the second or the third candle.

Fig. Down Gap Side By Side

10) Bearish Tri Star

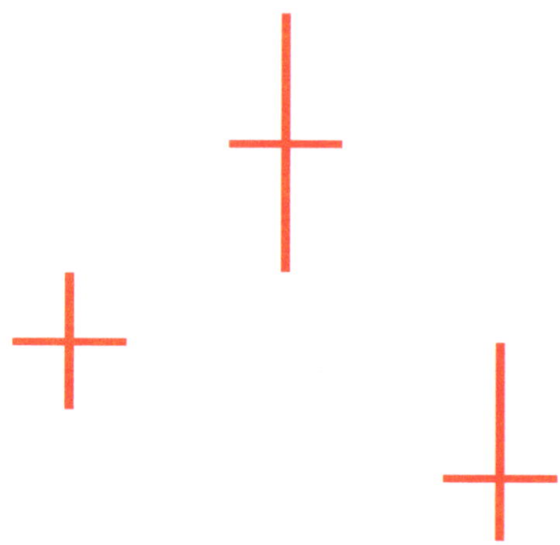

Fig. Bearish Tri Star

The Bearish tri star is a rare candlestick pattern that can indicate a bearish reversal after an uptrend. This candlestick pattern comprises three consecutive doji patterns. Here, the second doji appears after a gap up, and the third doji appears after a gap down.

How to trade a Bearish Tri Star?

One can look to enter a short position in the security when the price starts below the third Doji candle. Simultaneously, one should place the stop loss at the high of the second doji pattern.

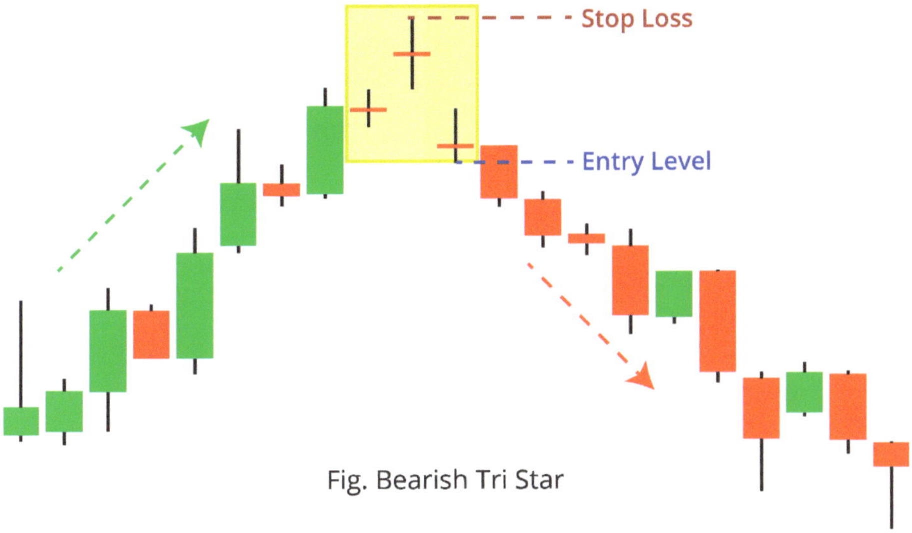

Fig. Bearish Tri Star

11) Bearish Stick Sandwich

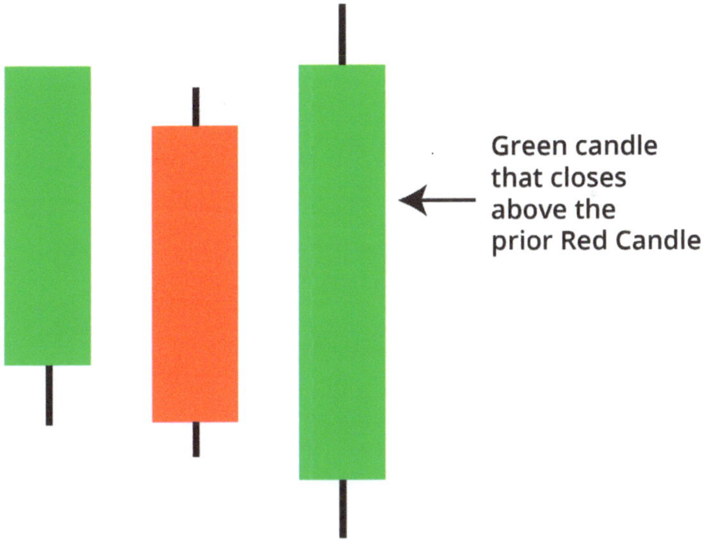

Fig. Bearish Stick Sandwich

The Bearish Stick Sandwich is a candlestick pattern that suggests a reversal after an uptrend. Here, the second candle is a red candle which is sandwiched between the two green candles. This candlestick pattern resembles the shape of a sandwich and is bearish in nature.

The bearish stick sandwich pattern comprises the following three candles:

1. A large green candle, which is a part of the uptrend
2. A small red candle
3. Another green candle that opens below the prior red candle.

The appearance of the red candlestick in this pattern indicates the entrance of the sellers in the security suggesting a potential bearish trend reversal.

How to trade a Bearish Stick Sandwich?

To trade this candlestick pattern, wait for another red candle to close below the third candle of the pattern to confirm the entry. One can enter a short position in the security when the price starts trading below the confirmation candle. The stop-loss for this trade should be kept at the high of the candlestick pattern.

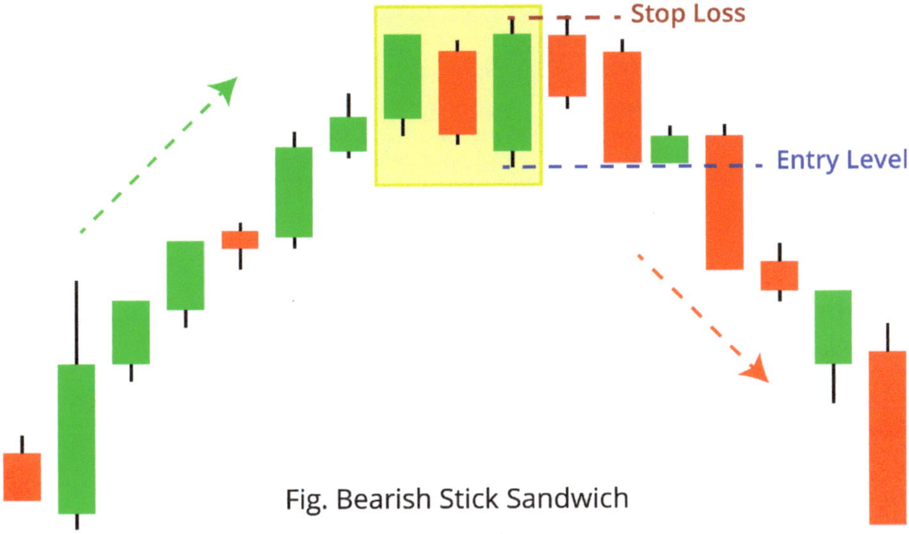

Fig. Bearish Stick Sandwich

BULLISH MULTI CANDLESTICK PATTERN

The Bullish Multi Candlestick Pattern consists of four or more consecutive candlestick patterns. These candle patterns are inherently bullish in nature, and the traders can take long positions based on these patterns.

1) Bullish Hikkake

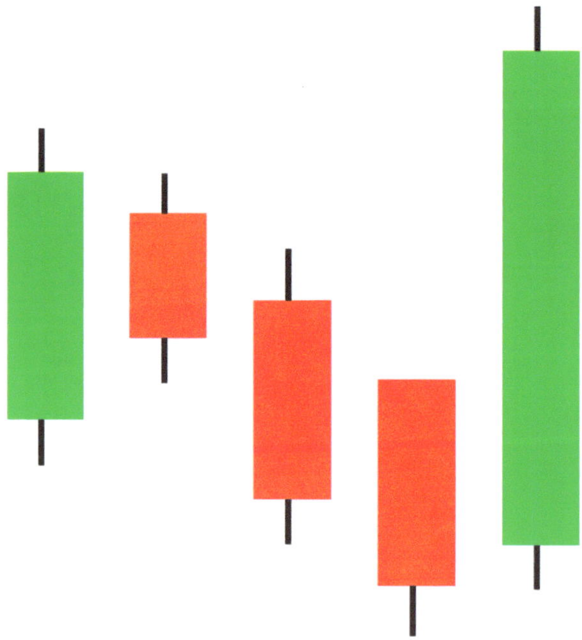

Fig. Bullish Hikkake

The bullish hikkake is a candlestick pattern that indicates a short-term reversal towards the uptrend. This candlestick pattern comprises the following candles:

1. The first two candles form an inside candlestick pattern or a harami pattern where the first candle completely overshadows the body of the second candle.
2. The third candle has a lower high and lower low compared to the second candle.
3. The fourth closes below the third candle.
4. The final candle is a green candle that closes above the high of the second candle.

This pattern suggests that the buyers are taking control, and the security may likely reverse upwards.

How to Trade a Bullish Hikkake Pattern?

One can enter a long position in the bullish hikkake pattern when the price starts trading above the high of the entire pattern. The Stop-loss for this trade should be kept at the low of the candlestick pattern.

Fig. Bullish Hikkake

2) Bullish Three Line Strike

Fig. Bullish Three Line Strike

Bullish three line strike pattern is a bullish continuation pattern that occurs in the middle of an uptrend. This candlestick pattern comprises of the following candles:

1. The first three candles are green where every candle closes higher than the prior candle.
2. A red candle that opens higher than the prior candle's high and closes below the first candle's low.

This pattern indicates that the uptrend is still intact, but the buyers booking their profits has caused a pullback in the security.

How to trade a Bullish Three Line Strike Pattern?

One can enter a long position in the bullish three line strike pattern when the price of the security starts trading above the high of the red (fourth) candle. The stop-loss for this trade should be kept near the low of the fourth candle.

Fig. Bullish Three Line Strike

3) Bullish Mat Hold

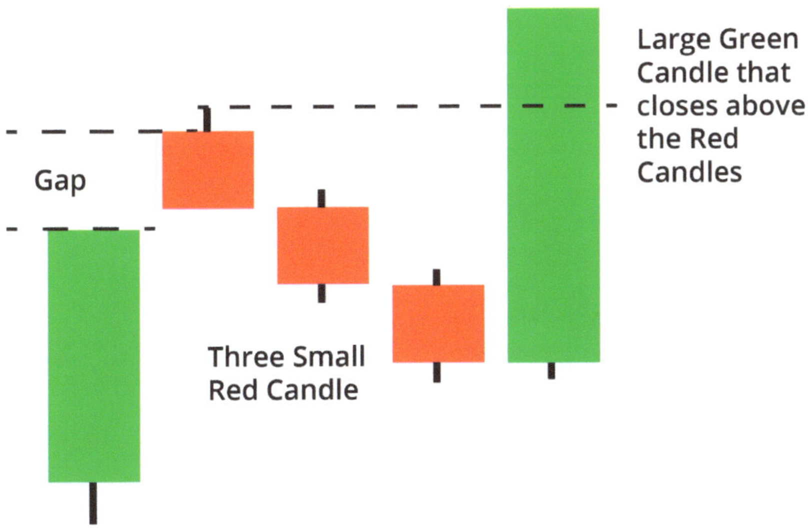

Fig. Bullish Mat Hold

The bullish mat hold pattern is a five-candlestick continuation pattern that forms in the middle of an uptrend. This candlestick pattern comprises of the following candles:

1. A large green candle that is a part of the uptrend
2. Next comes a gap up opening above the close of the green candle, followed by three small red candles that close above the opening price of the first green candle
3. A large green candle that closes above the red candles.

This pattern suggests that the buyers have regained control after the slight pullback in the market.

How to trade a Bullish Mat Hold Pattern?

One can enter a long position in the Bullish Mat Hold Pattern when the price of the security starts trading above the high of the fifth candle. The stop-loss for this trade should be kept below the low of the fifth candle.

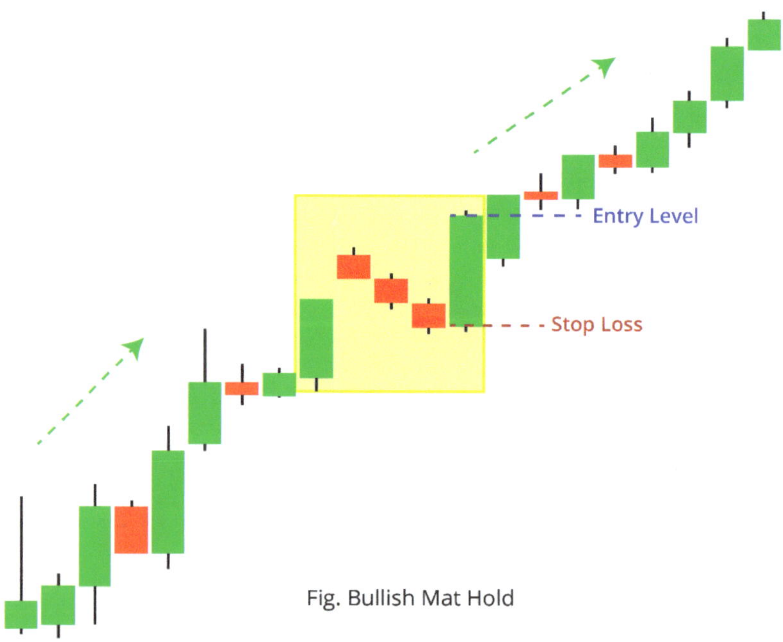

Fig. Bullish Mat Hold

4) Ladder Bottom

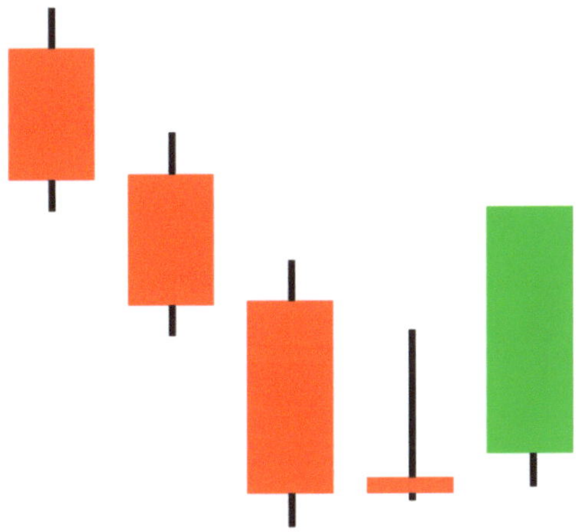

Fig. Ladder Bottom

The ladder bottom is a rare bullish pattern that indicates a reversal after a downtrend. This candlestick pattern comprises of the following candles:

1. The first three candles are red candles where each candle closes below the prior candle
2. The Fourth candle is a short-bodied red candle with a long upper wick.
3. The fifth candle is a large green candle that opens gap-up closes above the high of the fourth candle.

The formation of this pattern suggests that the sellers have been exhausted, which has allowed the buyers to take control of the security.

How to Trade a Ladder Bottom Pattern?

One can enter a long position in the Ladder Bottom Pattern when the price of the security starts trading above the fifth candle.

The stop-loss for this trade should be kept below the low of the pattern.

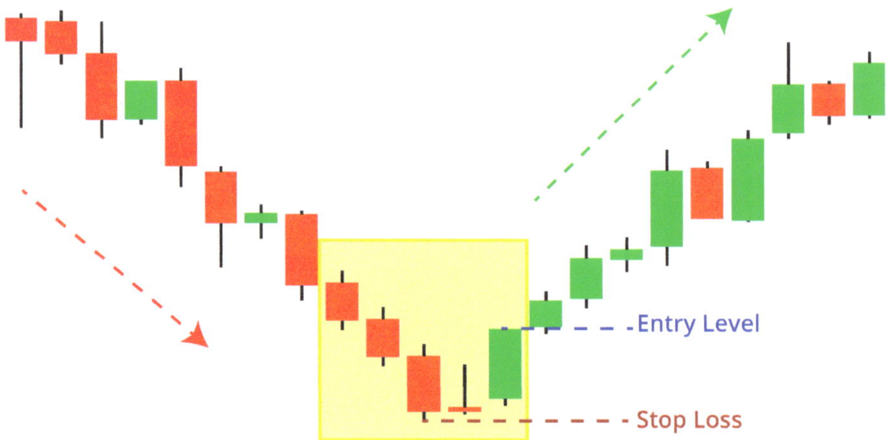

Fig. Ladder Bottom

5) Three Rising Method

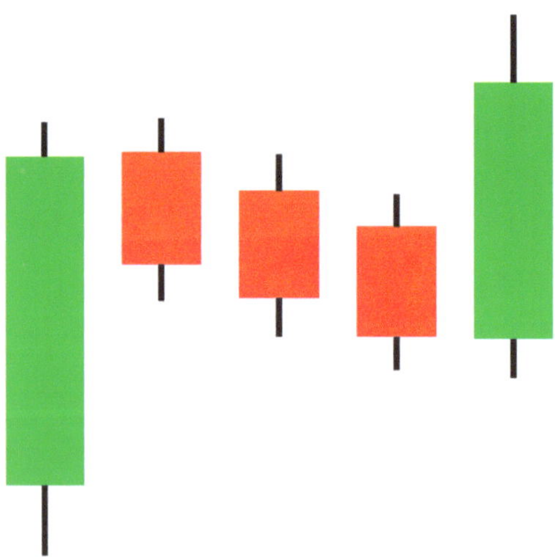

Fig. Three Rising Method

Three Rising Methods is a bullish continuation pattern that appears in the middle of an uptrend. This candlestick pattern comprises the following candles:

1. First candle is a large green candle, which is a part of the uptrend
2. The next three consecutive candles are red candles that close within the low and high of the first green candle
3. Final candle is a large green candle that closes significantly above the high of the first green candle.

The appearance of this pattern suggests that bulls are back in control after a brief period of consolidation and, hence, a resumption of the bullish trend.

How to trade a Three Rising Method Pattern?

One can enter a long position in the Three Rising Method Pattern when the price of the security starts trading above the high of the fifth green candle. The stop-loss for this trade should be kept near the low of the first candle in order to avoid early stopping out.

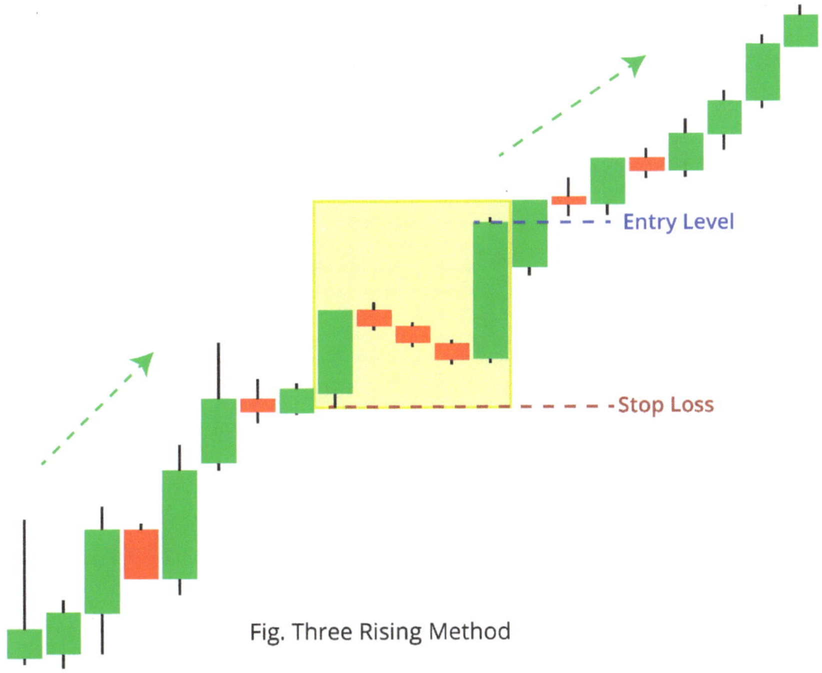

Fig. Three Rising Method

6) Bullish Breakaway Pattern

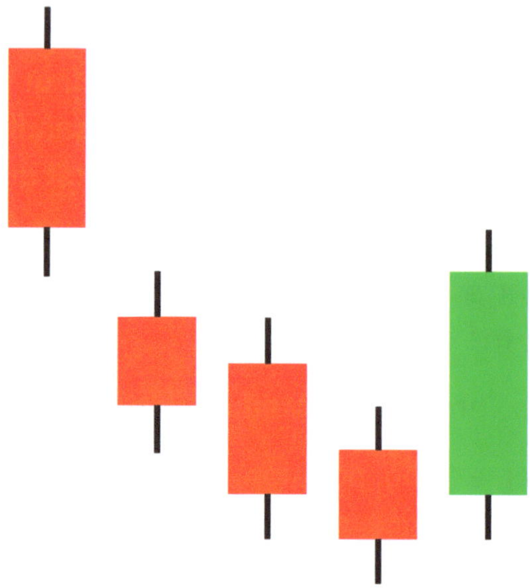

Fig. Bullish Breakaway Pattern

A Bullish Breakaway Pattern is a candlestick pattern that indicates a bullish reversal after a downtrend. This pattern comprises the following candles:

1. The first candle is a large red candle.
2. Next comes a gap down red candle that opens below the closing price of the large red candle, followed by two small red candles.
3. The final candle is a large green candle that opens with a positive gap up and breaks out above the previous three red candles.

The appearance of this pattern suggests that the sellers are losing control and the buyers have gained momentum in the market.

How to Trade a Bullish Breakaway Pattern?

One can enter a long position in the Bullish Breakaway Pattern when the price of the security starts trading above the high of the fifth green candle. The stop-loss for this trade should be kept below the low of the pattern.

Fig. Bullish Breakaway Pattern

BEARISH MULTI CANDLESTICK PATTERN

In this chapter, we will discuss the Bearish Multi Candlestick Patterns, their characteristics and how they are identified and used. The Bearish Multi Candlestick Pattern consists of four or more consecutive candlesticks and is bearish in nature. The traders can take short positions based on these patterns.

1) Bearish Hikkake

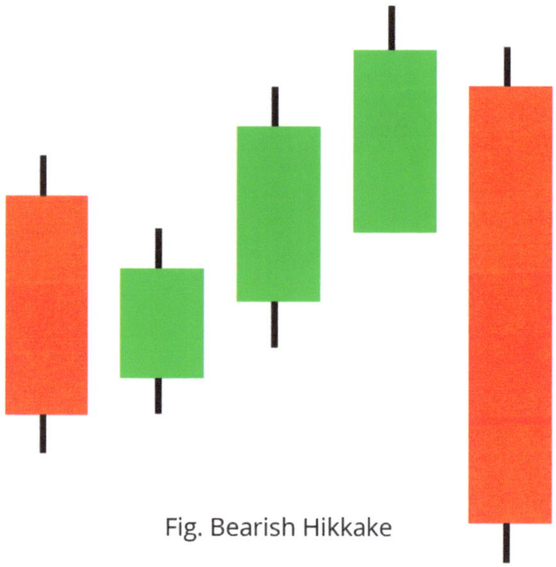

Fig. Bearish Hikkake

The bearish hikkake is a Multi candlestick pattern that indicates a short-term reversal towards the downtrend. This candlestick pattern comprises the following candles:

1. The first two candles are an inside candlestick pattern or a harami pattern where the first candle completely overshadows the body of the second candle.
2. The third candle has a higher high and higher low compared to the second candle.
3. The fourth closes above the third candle.
4. The final is a red candle that closes below the low of the previous candles.

This pattern suggests that the sellers are taking control, and the security may likely reverse downwards.

How to Trade a Bearish Hikkake Pattern?

One can enter a short position in the bearish hikkake pattern when the final candle closes below the low of the first candle. The Stop-loss for this trade should be kept at the high of the candlestick pattern.

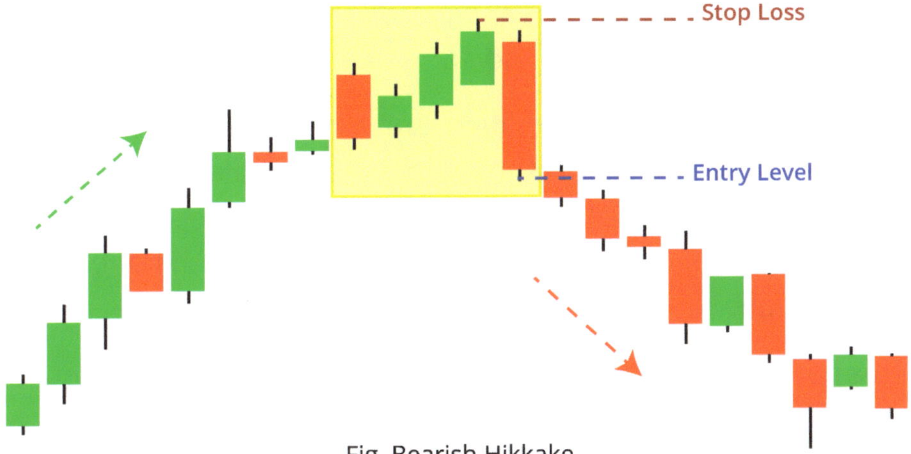

Fig. Bearish Hikkake

2) Bearish Three Line Strike

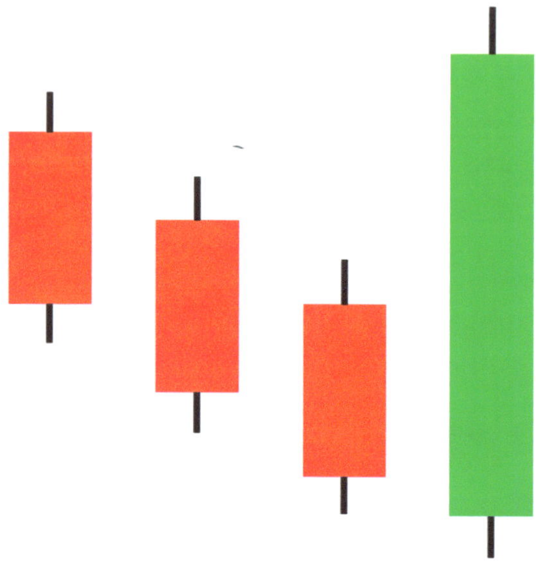

Fig. Bearish Three Line Strike

The Bearish three-line strike pattern is a downward continuation pattern that occurs in the middle of a downtrend. It is a rare multi-candlestick pattern and comprises the following candles:

1. The first three candles are red candles, where each candle closes lower than the prior candle.
2. The fourth candle is a green candle that opens lower to the prior candle's low and closes above the first candle's high.

This pattern indicates that the bearish sentiment has temporarily halted, but the security may decline further.

How to trade a Bearish Three Line Strike Pattern?

One can enter a short position in the bearish three line strike pattern when the price of the security starts trading below the low of the fourth candle of the pattern. The stop-loss for this trade should be kept near the high of the fourth candle.

Fig. Bearish Three Line Strike

3) Bearish Mat Hold

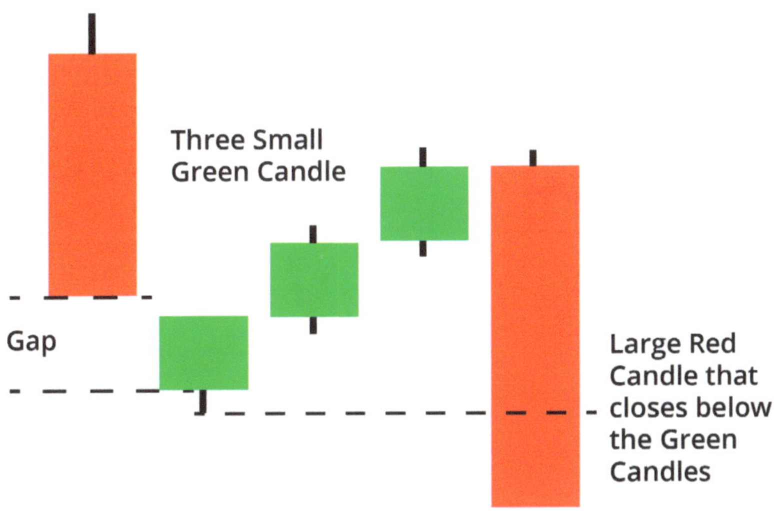

Fig. Bearish Mat Hold

The bearish mat hold pattern is a five-candlestick continuation pattern that forms in the middle of a downtrend. This candlestick pattern comprises of the following candles:

1. A large red candle that is a part of the current downtrend
2. A gap down opening below the close of the red candle followed by three green candles that close below the opening price of the first red candle.
3. A large red candle that closes below the low of the earlier three green candles.

This pattern suggests that the sellers have regained control after the slight pullback in the market.

How to trade a Bearish Mat Hold Pattern?

One can enter a short position in the bearish Mat Hold Pattern when the price of the security starts trading below the low of the fifth candle. The stop-loss for this trade should be kept near the high of the fifth candle.

Fig. Bearish Mat Hold

4) Ladder Top

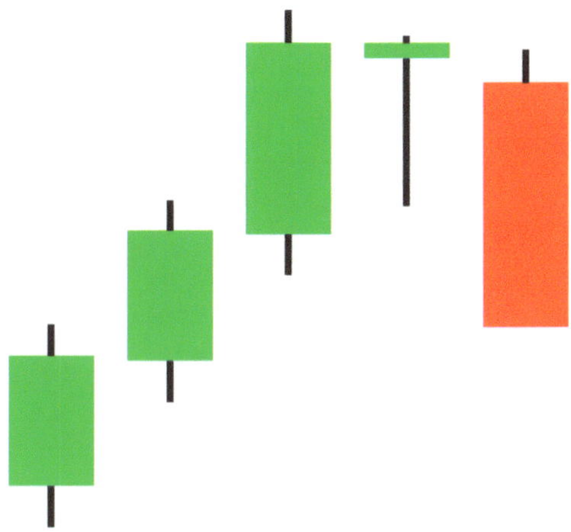

Fig. Ladder Top

The ladder top is a rare bearish pattern that indicates a reversal after an uptrend. This candlestick pattern comprises of the following candles:

1. The first three candles are green candles, with each closing above the prior candles
2. The Fourth candle is a short-bodied green candle with a long lower wick.
3. Fifth candle is a large red candle that opens gap-down and closes below the low of the fourth candle.

The formation of this pattern suggests that the buyers have been exhausted and, hence, has allowed the sellers to take control of the security.

How to Trade a Ladder Top Pattern?

One can enter a short position in the Ladder Bottom Pattern when the price of the security starts trading below the fifth candle. The stop-loss for this trade should be kept above the high of the pattern.

Fig. Ladder top

5) Three Falling Method

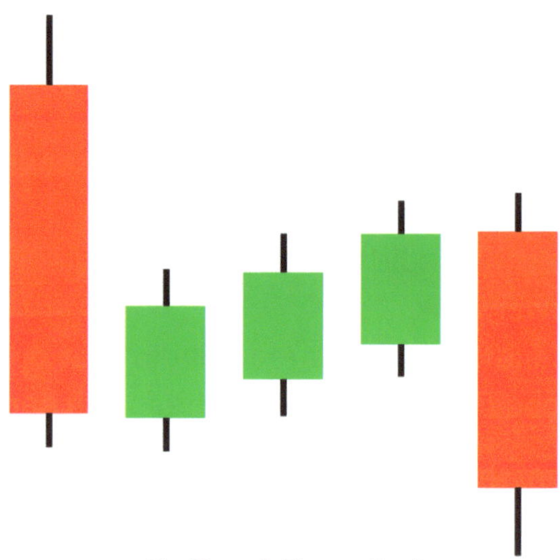

Fig. Three Falling method

Three Falling Methods is a bearish continuation pattern that appears in the middle of a downtrend. This candlestick pattern comprises the following candles:

1. The first candle is a large red candle, which is a part of the current downtrend
2. The next three candles are consecutive green candles that close within the low and high of the first red candle
3. The final candle is a large red candle that closes lower than the low of the first candle.

The appearance of this pattern suggests that the sellers have regained control in the security after a brief period of consolidation.

How to Trade a Three Falling Method Pattern?

One can enter a short position in the Three Falling Method Pattern when the price of the security starts trading below the low of the fifth red candle. The stop-loss for this trade should be kept near the high of the pattern to avoid premature stopping out.

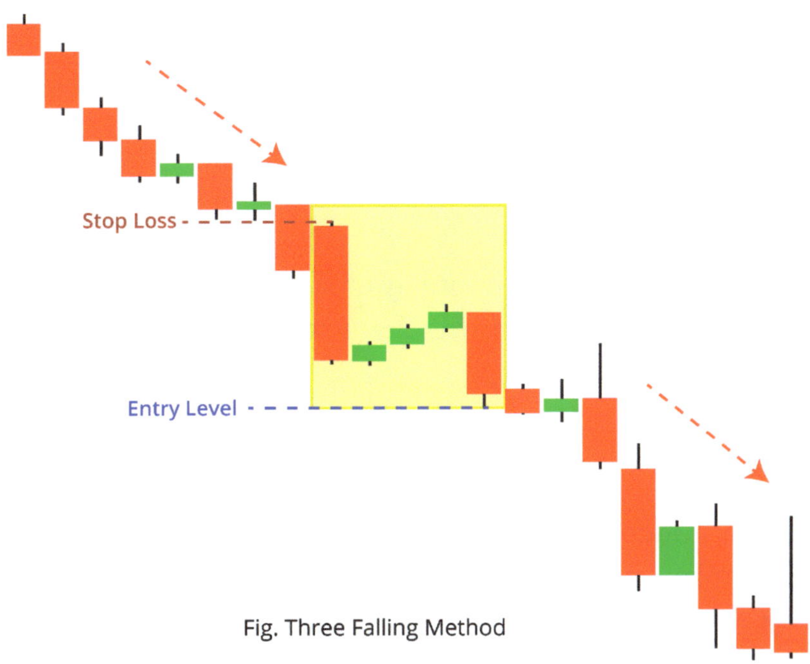

Fig. Three Falling Method

6) Bearish Breakaway Pattern

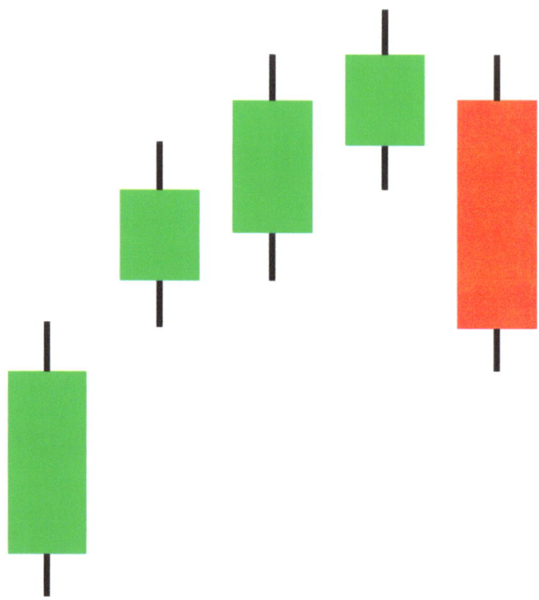

Fig. Bearish Breakaway Pattern

A Bearish Breakaway is a candlestick pattern that indicates a bearish reversal after an uptrend. This pattern comprises the following candles:

1. The first candle is a large green candle.
2. The next candle is green and opens at a gap up above the closing price of the first green candle and is followed by two small green candles.
3. A final candle is a large red candle that opens gap down and closes below the low of the fourth candle.

The appearance of this pattern suggests that the buyers are losing control and the sellers have gained momentum in the market and potentially a bearish reversal.

How to Trade a Bearish Breakaway Pattern?

One can trade the bearish Breakaway Pattern when the price of the security starts trading below the low of the fifth red candle. The stop-loss for this trade should be kept above the high of the pattern.

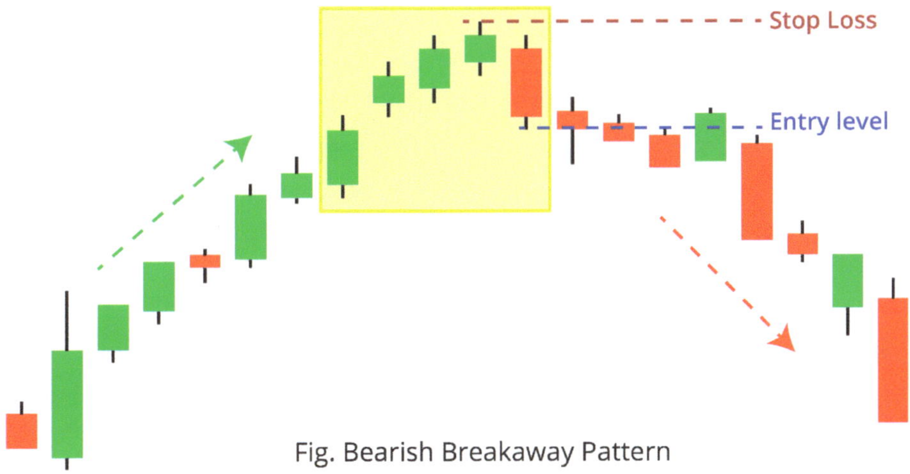

Fig. Bearish Breakaway Pattern

HOW TO BOOK PROFITS AFTER ENTERING A TRADE?

So far, we have discussed the composition of various candlestick patterns, as well as how to enter trades for each of them and where to put your stop losses. However, we have not yet discussed the concept of setting a profit target or when exactly you should book profit and exit your trades.

There are generally four methods for booking profits in a trade, and these apply to all the candlestick patterns we have covered thus far. These include booking profits based on the risk-to-reward ratio, support and resistance levels, using trailing stop-loss, and finally, looking into the size of the chart patterns.

1) Profit Booking based on Risk-to-Reward Ratio

Risk-to-reward is a simple method of determining the profits based on the amount of losses you are willing to incur in a trade. This ratio tells us how much profit we expect to make for every rupee we are willing to risk. Disciplined traders maintain their Risk-to-reward ratio in every trade that they take.

For instance, If we are willing to take the risk of Rs 500 in a trade and the potential profit we expect is Rs1000, then the risk-to-reward ratio for this trade will be 1:2. Similarly if the risk appetite is Rs.500 and the profit expectation is Rs 1,500, the risk-to-reward ratio becomes 1:3.

To determine the profit target on trades based on Risk to risk reward ratio, you adhere to the following steps:

Step 1: Decide risk-to-reward per trade. This ratio can vary and be set at 1:1, 1:2, 1:3, and so on, depending on how confident you are about the trade. If you have a high level of conviction about a particular trade, you may want to consider setting a higher risk-to-reward ratio and vice versa.

Step 2: When you enter a position in the security in the trade, set a stop loss on the desired level. This level can be based on the level of your risk tolerance.

Step 3: The final step is setting the profit target for the trade. Suppose you are entering an equity at a price of Rs 100. Here, you are setting up a stop loss of 20 points i.e. willing to exit the trade if the price goes to 80 or below. If you want a risk-to-reward of 1:1, then your profit target should also be 20 points, and you should exit a favourable trade only when the price goes to 120 or above.

2) Profit Booking Based on the level of support and resistance:

As discussed in the initial chapters, support and resistance are the levels where the price of security has reversed in the past. These levels can be used to book profits in the trade as the uptrend or downtrend may change on these crucial levels.

If a long position has been entered in security after the downtrend, the profit target for this trade should be the immediate level of resistance. Similarly, when a short position has been entered, the immediate level of support can be considered as the profit target.

Fig. Profit Booking Strategies

3) Profit Booking based on trailing stop-loss

Trailing stop-loss is the method of continuously adjusting your stop-loss when the security is moving in your favour.

Here, you set your initial stop-loss while entering the trade, and as the security starts moving in your direction, you shift the stop-loss, which allows you to lock in profits while allowing you to benefit further.

For example, let's say that you entered a long trade at Rs 100 and set the initial stop loss at Rs 80. Now when the price goes in your favour and moves to 125, you moved the stop-loss to 105. Using this approach, you have trailed your stop loss.

In this profit booking method, you shift the stop-loss only when the security moves in your favour and not against it.

4) Profit booking based on the size of the Charts and candlestick patterns

This is the method of profit booking that involves setting targets based on the size of the candlestick patterns and charts. While trading based on technicals, you may see the formation of different types of chart patterns like Cup and Handle Pattern, Double top, Double bottom and other patterns. Here, you can define the targets based on the pattern's characteristics and nature. In the upcoming chapter on' Trading with Chart patterns', we'll discuss in depth about when you should exit the trade when you see these chart patterns.

Similarly, you can also look into the candlestick patterns and define the target based on its size and height.

Generally, the idea of where to book profit will come to you with practice and experience. As you get more experience, you will have your own ideas on when you should book and when you should hold to target for bigger profits. Nonetheless, the four techniques discussed above are used by most trades to define their profit target.

TRENDLINES AND HOW TO DRAW THEM?

A trendline is a distinctive line drawn on the charts by connecting a series of opening prices, closing prices, and the highs and lows of security. These trendlines provide traders with a general direction of the trend in the market.

In addition to providing a general trend direction, trendlines can also be used as diagonal support and resistance lines when markets trend in a certain direction. These lines are also helpful in the formation of various chart patterns that can help traders make informed decisions when trading in the market.

In general, trendlines can be categorised into two ways: The upward or support trendline and the downward or resistance trendlines

Upward or Support Trendline

An upward or support trendline is a line formed when the price of the security is trending in an upward direction. Here, you should be able to connect the low prices of the security for more than two consecutive points with the help of a single line.

The lows created for an upward trendline should be higher than its prior low as the price of the security progresses forward. The more times the price touches and bounces off the trendline, the upward trendline gets a better conviction of the strength.

As the name suggests, this line acts as a support level for the security and can create a good buying opportunity. When the price of the security touches and bounces back from the upward trendline, one can open a long position in the security and place a stop loss a few points below the entry-level.

When the price of the security breaks below the upward trendline, it is an indication that the bullish trend has come to an end.

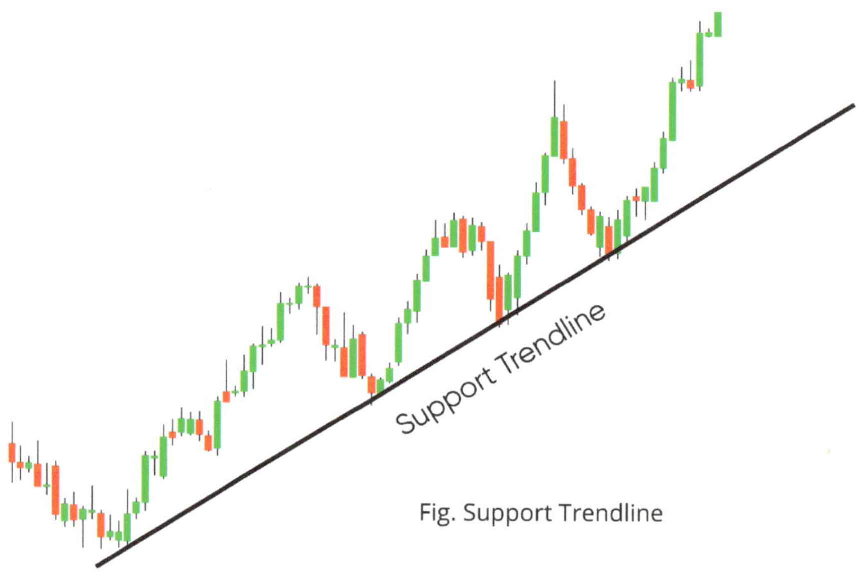

Fig. Support Trendline

Downward or Resistance Trendline

A downward or resistance trendline is a line formed when the price of the security is trending in a downward direction. Here, you should be able to connect the high prices of the security for more than two consecutive points with the help of a single line.

The highs created for a downward trendline should be lower than its prior highs as the price of the security progresses forward. The strength of the downward trendline gets better conviction when the price touches and reverses from the trendline more times.

As the name suggests, this line acts as a resistance level for the security and can create a good selling (shorting) opportunity in the security. When the price of the security touches and bounces back from the downward trendline, one can open a short position in the security and place a stop loss a few points above the entry level.

When the price of the security breaks above the upward trendline, it is an indication that the bearish trend has come to an end.

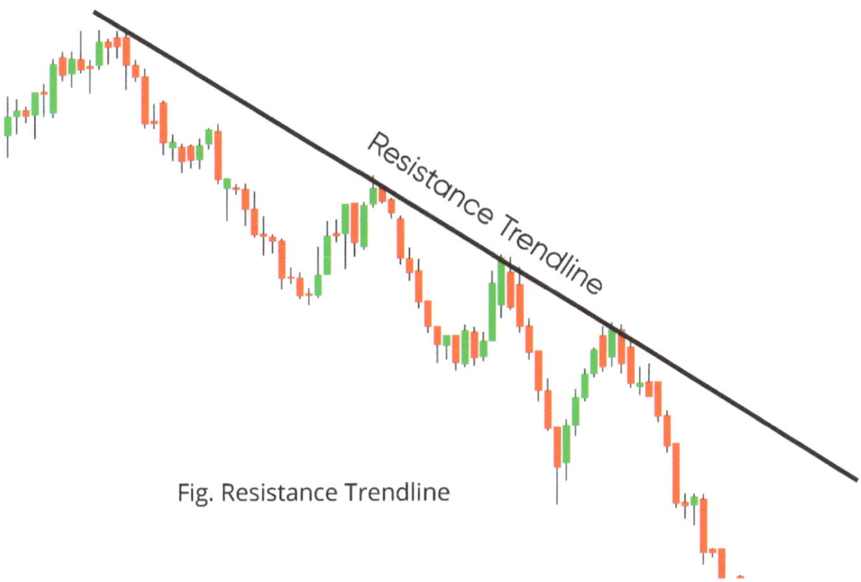

Fig. Resistance Trendline

How to Draw Trend Lines?

In order for a line to be considered as a strong trendline, it needs to be connected to three price points sloping in an upward or downward direction. Following are the steps to draw a trendline for security.

Initiating Point: This is the price point from which you start plotting the trendline of the security. This is the point from which you start drawing the line to identify the trend.

Confirmation Point: This is the second price point on the chart that helps constitute a trendline. It is the price point where the security has bounced back up or down. This is the point at which you extend the line from the initiating point and extend it further throughout the future chart which helps you form a trendline.

Validation Point: This is the final price point in the chart which confirms the validity of the trendline. While the two points are connected to each other on a speculative basis and extended further in the future, the third point helps you confirm the trend that exists in security.

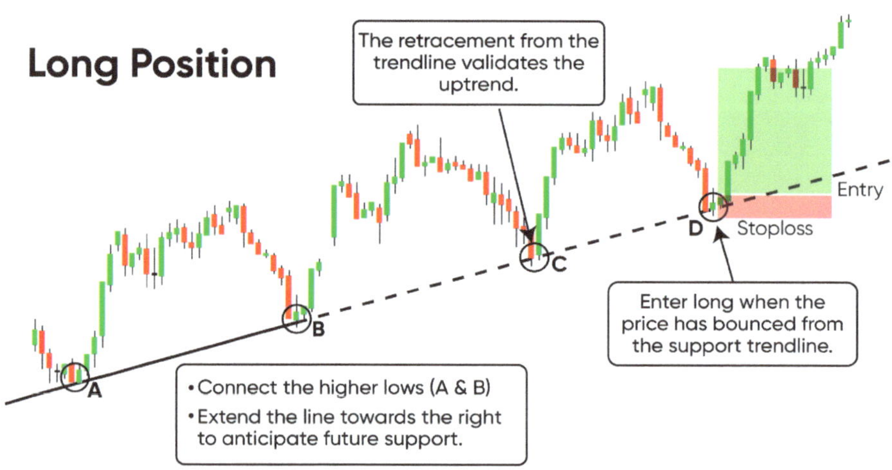

Fig. Guideline to Draw Support Trendline

Once you have identified this point, you can place your respective trades and continue to do so as the security bounces from these trendlines.

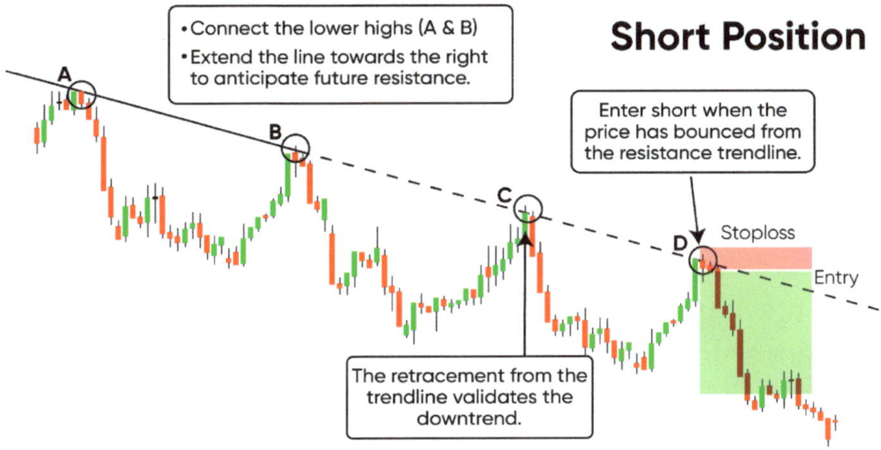

Fig. Guideline to Draw Resistance Trendline

TRADING WITH CHANNELS

In the previous chapters, we have discussed about Support and resistance along with drawing trendlines. In this chapter, you will learn the next important charting concept which is known as 'Channels'.

A Channel pattern is the range of parallel support and resistance lines between which a security is trading. These are formed by joining the lows and highs trending in the same direction. Here, the lower line of the channel acts as a support level while the upper trend line acts as a resistance for security.

These channels might slope upwards, downwards or sideways, and based on this they are categorised into ascending, descending, and rectangle channel patterns. Let us understand the three of these patterns in detail

1) Rectangular Channel

A rectangle channel pattern is a range of horizontal parallel lines within which a security is trading. This channel pattern indicates a period of consolidation in the market.

Here, the resistance line of the channel is formed by connecting at least two price points that have equal highs and the support line of the channel is formed by connecting at least two price points that have equal lows.

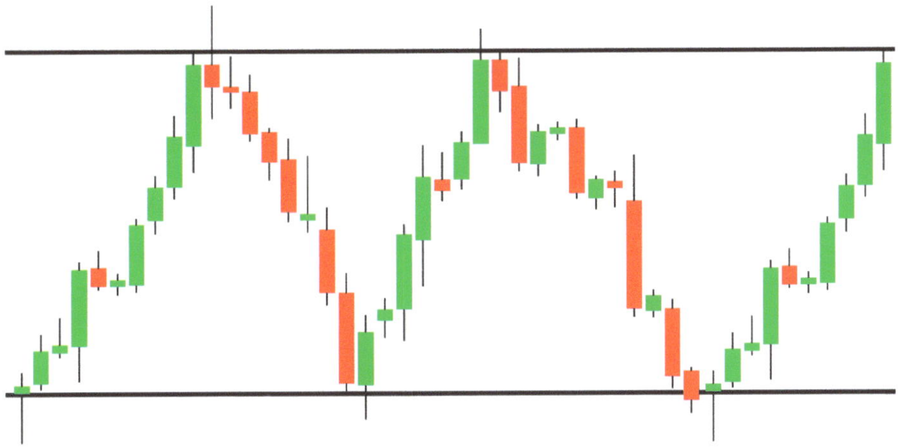

Fig. Rectangle Channel Pattern

2) Ascending Channel Pattern

An Ascending channel pattern is a range of upward-sloping parallel lines within which a security is trading. It is considered a bullish pattern as the buyers are pushing the price of the security gradually higher.

Here, the upper trendline of the channel is formed by connecting at least two price points when they are making higher highs and the lower trendline of the channel is also formed by connecting at least two price points when they are making higher lows.

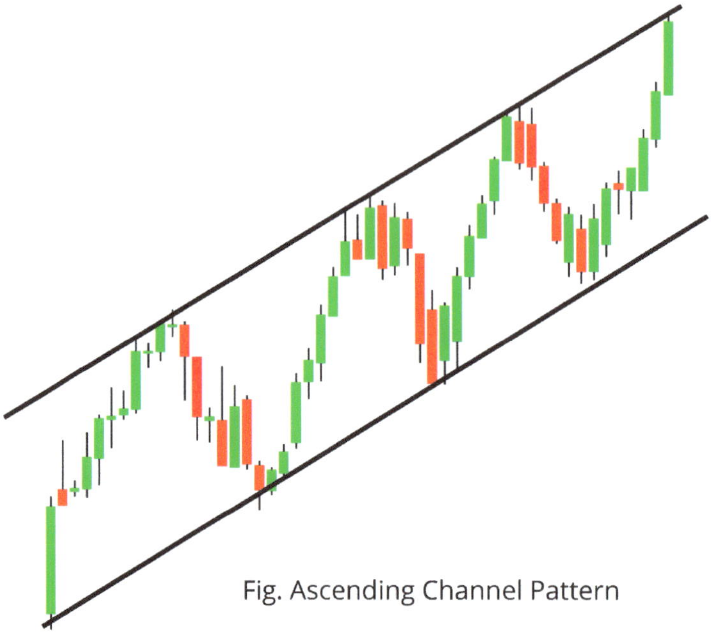

Fig. Ascending Channel Pattern

3) Descending Channel Pattern

An Descending channel pattern is a range of downward-sloping parallel lines within which a security is trading. It is considered a bearish pattern as the sellers are pushing the price of the security gradually lower.

Here, the upper trendline of the channel is formed by connecting at least two price points when they are making lower highs and the lower trendline of the channel is also formed by connecting at least two price points when they are making lower lows.

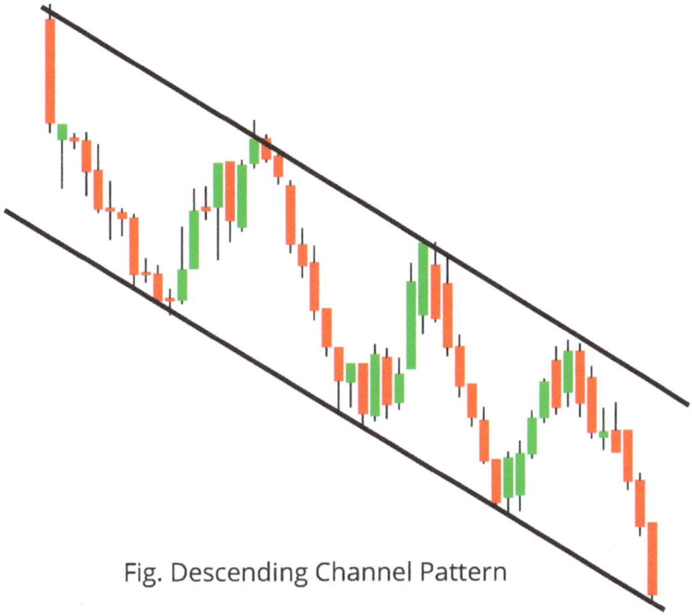

Fig. Descending Channel Pattern

How to Trade the Channel Patterns?

Once the upper trendline and the lower trendlines are formed in the above three channel patterns you can extend these lines further ahead in the chart to predict the future price trends and trade in the security.

All three channel patterns can be traded similarly, and there are three ways of doing so. Here are ways in which you can trade the channel patterns:

Trading with the Swing

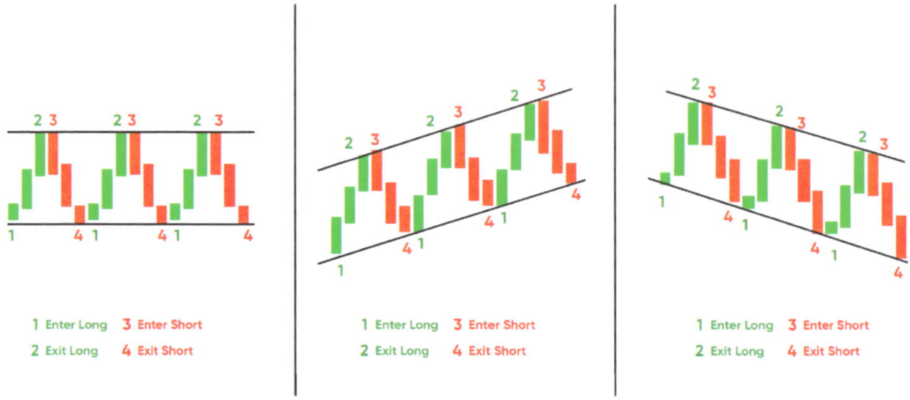

Fig. Trading channels with the swings

In this trading strategy, you enter a trade when the price is moving inside the channel formation.

Here, you can enter a long position when the price is near the lower trendline of the pattern and exit the position when the price starts reaching the upper trendline of the pattern. The stop loss for this trade should be placed a few points below the point of entry.

Similarly, you can enter a short position when the price is near the upper trendline of the pattern and square off the position when the price starts reaching the lower trendline of the pattern. The stop loss for this trade should be placed a few points above the point of entry.

Breakout on the Upside

Here, you can enter a trade when the price of the security moves beyond the upper trendline of the pattern. The breakout indicates a strong wave of buyers entering the security.

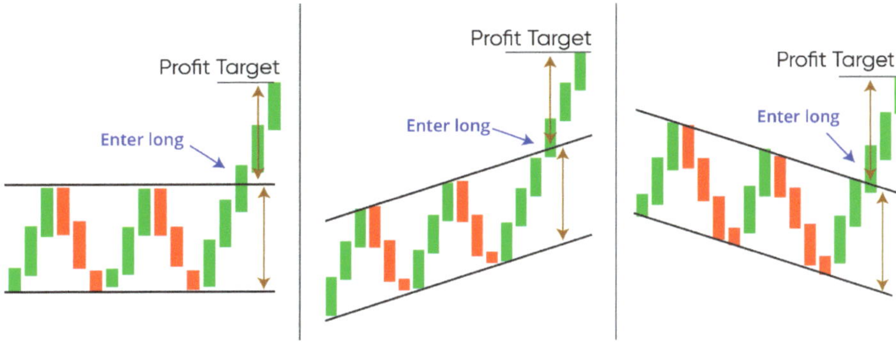

Fig. Trading channels during upside breakout

When a security breaks above the upper trendline, you can enter a long position in the trade, keeping the upper trendline as support and a trigger for stop loss. The profit target for this pattern can be taken to be the same as the height of the channel.

Breakout on the Downside

Here you can enter a trade when the price of the security moves below the lower trendline of the pattern. The breakout on the downside indicates that the sellers have entered the security.

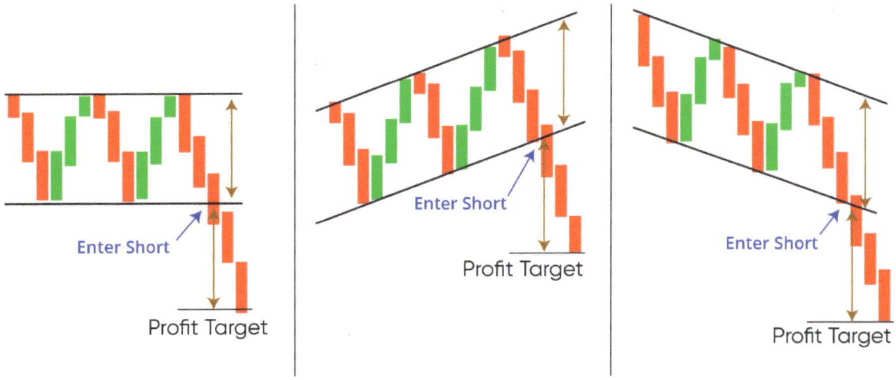

Fig. Trading Channels during Downside Breakout

When the security moves below the lower trendline, you can enter a short position in the trade, keeping the lower trendline as resistance and a trigger for stop loss. The profit target for this pattern should be the same as the height of the channel.

TRADING WITH GAPS

A gap opening is a break in the prices of the security that occurs between the closing and opening prices of two consecutive sessions. In simpler terms, if the security opens at the same price at which it closed in the last session, then there's no gapup but simply a continuation. On the other hand, if a security's opening price is different from the trading session of the previous closing price, it is called a Gap up or Gap down, based on where it is opening.

When a security has opened above the closing price of the previous trading session, it is considered a gap-up opening. When a security has opened below the closing price of the previous trading session, it is considered a gap-down opening.

A Gap opening indicates the likely interest of buyers and sellers in the market. A gap down in the market indicates the sellers have more interest, while a gap up indicates the buyers are showing more interest.

Gaps occur in different forms and are categorised into different types in the market. Here are the types of gap openings that can occur in a security.

1) Common Gaps

Common gaps, also known as trading gaps or area gaps, appear in security due to regular market pressure and do not require any special events to take place. These gaps are often small in size and tend to get filled quickly. Security tends to revert back to its previous levels only a few trading sessions after the occurrence of this type of gap.

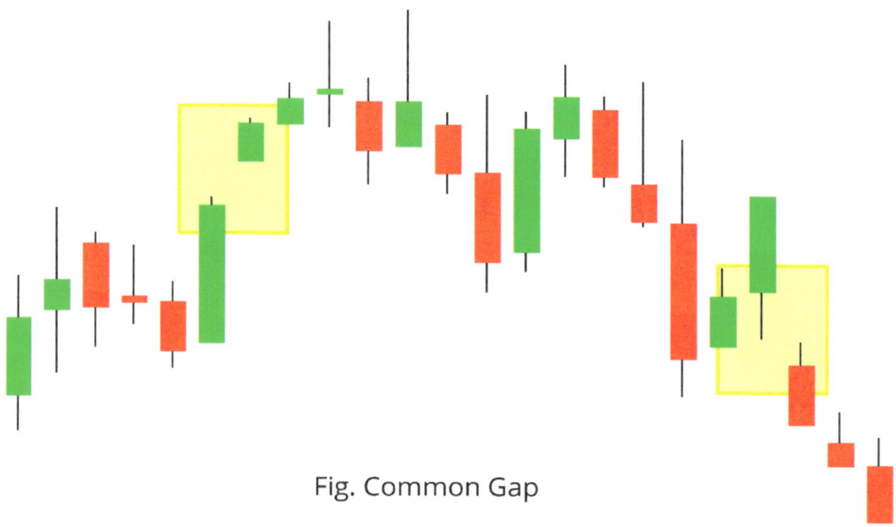

Fig. Common Gap

2) Breakaway Gaps

Breakaway gaps occur upon the end of a significant price trend and indicate the beginning of a new trend of security. It appears when the price of the security opens above a resistance area or below a support area from a well-established trading range through a gap. The occurrence of these gaps is usually accompanied by an inflow of high trading volumes, which indicates the conviction of the new trend.

A bullish breakaway gap occurs when the price opens above the previous day's closing price, which causes an end to the sideways movement in the security price and begins an upward trend.

A bearish breakaway gap occurs when a price opens below the previous day's closing price, which causes an end to the sideways movement in the security price and begins a downward trend.

Fig. Breakaway Gap

3) Exhaustion Gap

An exhaustion gap is an indication of the final stretch in the price of the security. It is a gap opening in the direction of the current trend and indicates the final attempt of the buyers or sellers to push the price in their favour. After the emergence of this gap, security tends to take a reversal in the opposite direction. The occurrence of these gaps are usually accompanied by lower trading volumes, indicating that the current trend is coming to an end.

A bullish exhaustion gap occurs when the price has opened a gap down during an existing downtrend, which is followed by a bullish reversal in the security.

A bearish exhaustion gap occurs when the price has opened gap up during an existing uptrend which is followed by a bearish reversal in the security.

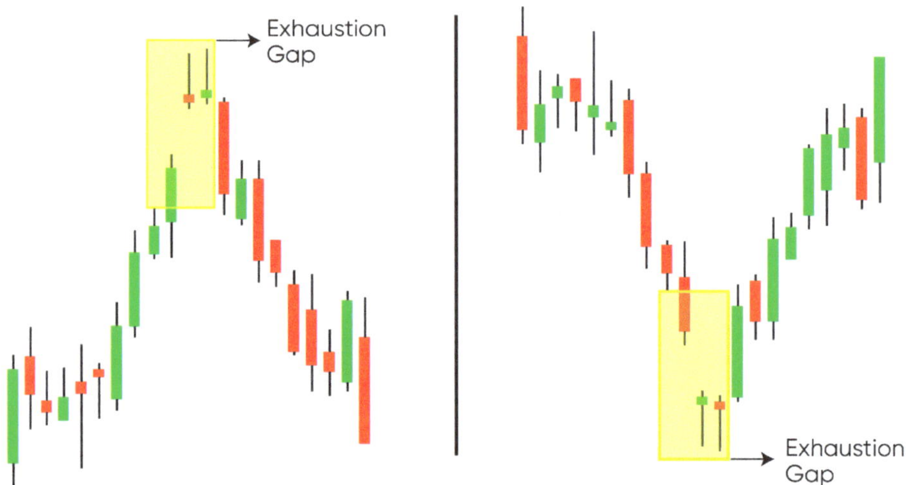

Fig. Exhaustion Gap

4) Continuation Gap

A continuation gap, also referred to as a runaway gap, appears in the direction of the existing trend and indicates that the trend is likely going to continue. This gap indicates that the buyers or sellers have a strong grip on the market.

When the security opens a gap up from an existing uptrend and continues in the upward direction, it is called a bullish continuation gap. This gap indicates that the buyers have a strong grip on the existing uptrend.

A bearish continuation gap is when the security opens a gap down from the existing downtrend and continues the downward trend. This gap indicates that the sellers have a strong grip on the existing downtrend.

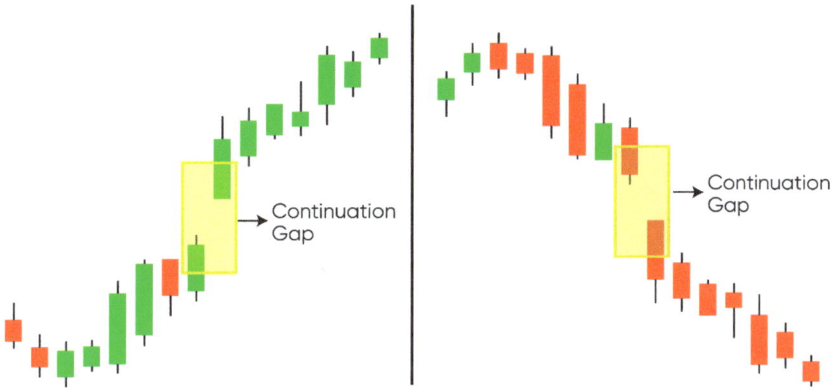

Fig. Continuation Gap

How to Trade Gaps?

Though the types of gaps that appear in the market are categorised into various, trading using these gaps can be a difficult task. A reason for saying this is that the type of gap can be confirmed only after the price has made its complete movement. By this time, it is often too late to take an entry into the market, due to which it is best to avoid trades using these gaps.

There are alternative methods to trade using market gaps, such as employing candlestick patterns, including thrusting, neck, and window patterns.

Another alternative strategy that you can use is the gap-filling concept. Generally, when security makes a huge gap opening in the direction of the prevailing trend, it tends to fill up the gap during the next sessions. This can be due to a large number of market participants taking up a buying position or a huge number of participants squaring of their positions.

When a security makes a huge gap up opening, it tends to fall to the levels of the previous day's closing price. This is a good opportunity to enter a short position in security while simultaneously placing a stoploss a few points above the entry level.

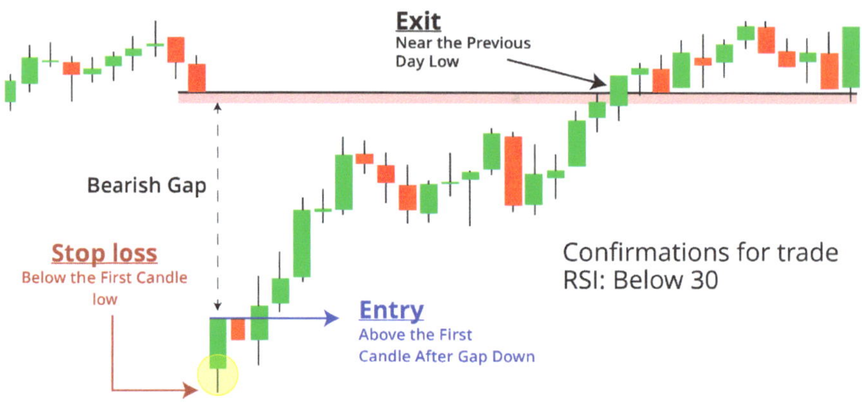

Fig. Gap Filling After Gap Down

When a security makes a huge gap down opening, it tends to rise to the levels of the previous day's closing price to fill the gap. This is a good opportunity to enter a long position in the security while simultaneously placing a stop loss a few points below the entry level.

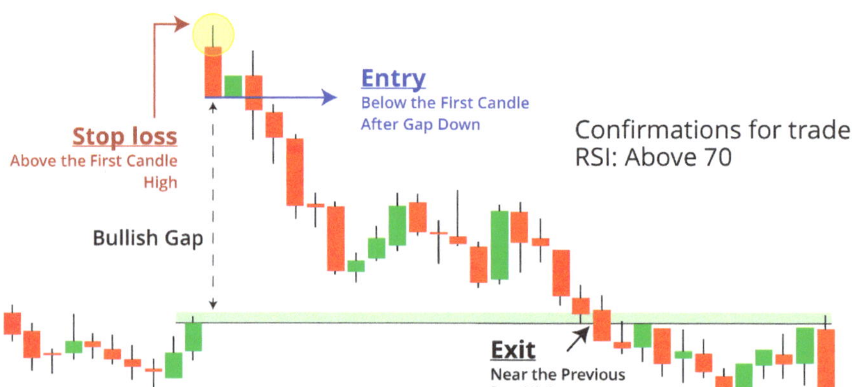

Fig. Gap Filling After Gap Up

Nonetheless, as discussed earlier, gap trading is not as simple as compared to other chart patterns trading. If the market gaps up 100 points next day, even if you had bullish view, you would have missed the opportunity. In addition, taking contra trade to fill the gap may require quick execution and exit strategy.

TRADING WITH CHART PATTERNS

In this chapter, we will discuss a few of the most important and frequently used chart patterns while trading. Here, we will discuss how these chart patterns are identified and how to trade them once identified. We'll discuss the general entry point, stop loss and profit target while trading these chart patterns. Let's get started.

Please note that in the chart patterns discussed below, we have explained the ideal profit target and where one should exit the trade. However, it is important to keep in mind that if there are any immediate support or resistance levels next to the pattern, it is recommended to book profits at those levels instead of waiting for the mathematical profit targets.

1) Ascending Triangle Pattern

An Ascending triangle is a bullish continuation pattern that is formed when the price of a security makes higher lows which is followed by a downward reversal from a horizontal level of support.

A breakout above the triangle signals that the bulls are gaining momentum and is an indication of a further uptrend in the market. The best scenario for this pattern to appear is during an uptrend in the market.

How to trade using the Ascending Channel Pattern?

Entry Level: When the price of the security breaks above the resistance level of the pattern, you should take a long position in the security as it suggests the continuation of the uptrend.

Profit Target: The profit target for this pattern should match the distance between the lowest point in the pattern and the resistance level of the pattern. When the price matches the calculated distance, one can book profits from the trade.

Stop Loss: The resistance line of the ascending triangle pattern should act as a trigger stop-loss while trading using this pattern. One should place a stop loss a few points below the resistance line of the pattern to avoid early stopping out.

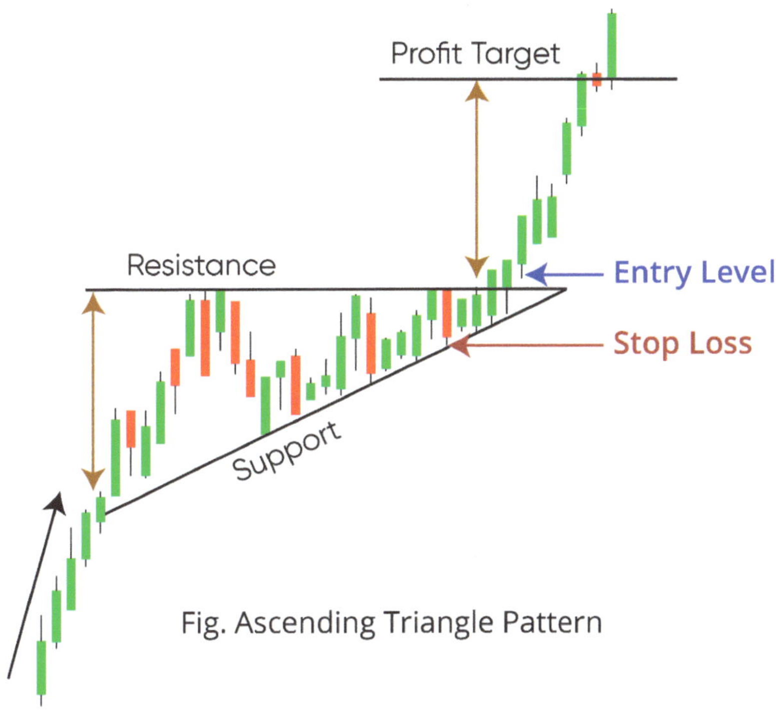

Fig. Ascending Triangle Pattern

2) Descending Triangle Pattern

A Descending triangle is a bearish continuation pattern that is formed when the price of a security is making lower highs which is followed by an upward reversal from a horizontal level of support.

A breakdown below the triangle signals that the bears are gaining momentum and is an indication of a further downtrend in the market. The best scenario for this pattern to appear is during a downtrend in the market.

How to trade using the Descending Channel Pattern?

Entry Levels: When the price of the security breaks below the support level of the pattern, you should take a short position in the security as it suggests the continuation of the downtrend.

Profit Target: The profit target for this pattern should match the distance between the highest point in the pattern and the support level of the pattern or the immediate next support level. When the price matches the calculated distance, one can book profits from the trade.

Stop Loss: The support line of the descending triangle pattern should trigger stop-loss while trading using this pattern. One should place a stop-loss a few points above the support line of the pattern.

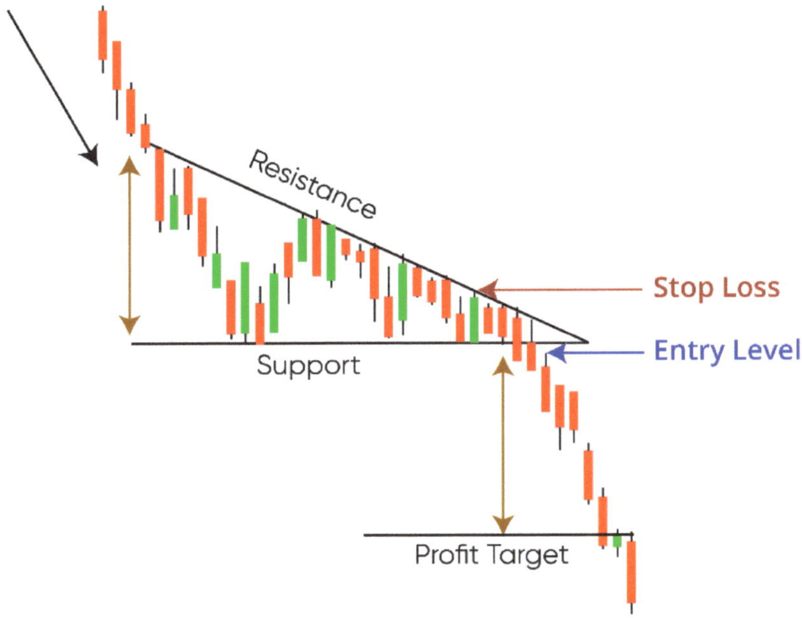

Fig. Descending Triangle Pattern

3) Falling Wedge Pattern

A falling wedge is a bullish reversal pattern that is formed when the price of the security forms lower highs and lower lows and the trend lines drawn converge as the price falls. The downward convergence in the upper and lower trendline indicates that the bears are losing momentum in the security and the price is likely to reverse from the existing trend.

How to trade using the Falling Wedge Pattern?

Entry Level: When the price of the security breaks above the upper trendline of the pattern, you should enter a long position in the security as it indicates a bullish reversal in the security.

Profit Target: The profit target for this pattern should be the immediate resistance level in the security or based according to the risk-to-reward ratio of the market participants.

Stop Loss: The upper trendline of the candlestick pattern should be the trigger for stop-loss while trading using this pattern. One should place a stop loss a few points below the upper trendline line of the pattern.

Fig. Falling Wedge Pattern

4) Rising Wedge Pattern

A Rising wedge is a bearish reversal pattern that is formed when the price of the security forms higher lows and higher highs and the trend lines drawn converge as the price rises. The upward convergence in the trendlines indicates that the bulls are losing momentum in the security, and the price is likely to reverse from the existing trend.

How to trade using the Rising Wedge Pattern?

Entry Level: When the price of the security breaks below the lower trendline of the pattern, one should enter a short position in the security as it indicates a bearish reversal in the security.

Profit Target: The profit target for this pattern should be the immediate support level in the security. The profit target can also be based according to the risk-to-reward ratio of the market participants.

Stop Loss: The lower trendline of the candlestick pattern should be the trigger for stop-loss while trading using this pattern. One should place a stop loss a few points above the lower trendline line of the pattern.

Fig. Rising Wedge Pattern

5) Double Top Pattern

A double top, also known as 'M' pattern, is a bearish reversal pattern that is formed when the price of the security makes two consecutive highs that are separated by a pullback in the centre which is the baseline or support level of the pattern. Here, the bulls tried to push the prices higher twice but failed.

This pattern indicates that the bullish momentum is weakening, and there might be a potential trend reversal in the security.

How to trade using the Double Top pattern?

Entry Level: When the price of the security breaks below the support line of the pattern that separates the two highs, you should enter a short position in the security as it indicates a bearish reversal in the security.

Profit Target: The profit target for this pattern should match the distance between the highest point and its support neckline of the pattern or the next immediate support level. When the price matches the calculated distance, one can book profits from the trade.

Stop Loss: The support line of the chart pattern should be the trigger for stop-loss while trading using this pattern. One should place a stop loss a few points above the support line of the pattern.

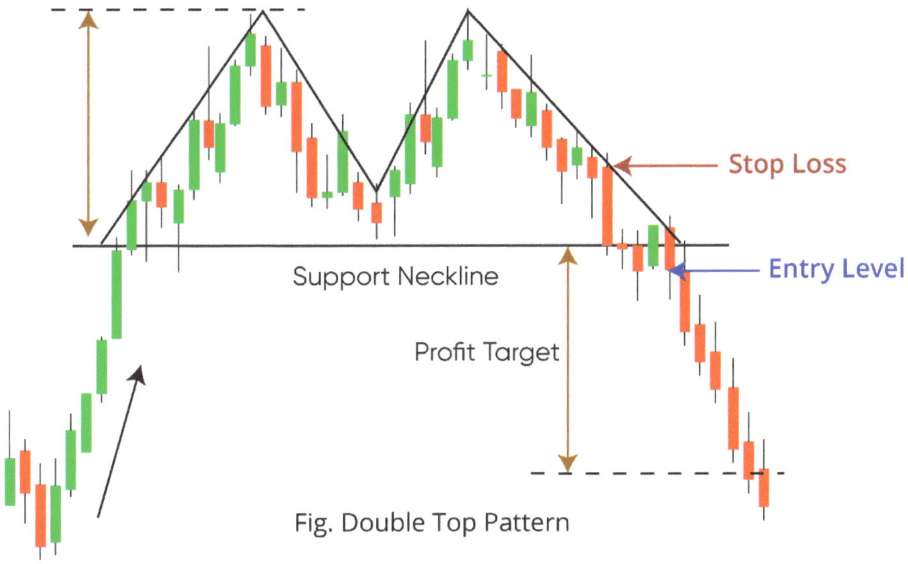

Fig. Double Top Pattern

6) Double Bottom Pattern

The Double Bottom, also known as W pattern, is a bullish reversal pattern that is formed when the price of the security reaches a low two consecutive times that are separated by a pullback in the centre, which is the baseline or resistance level of the pattern. Here, the bears tried to push the prices lower twice but failed.

This pattern indicates that the bearish momentum is weakening, and there might be a potential trend reversal in the security.

How to trade using the Double Bottom pattern?

Entry Level: When the price of the security breaks above the resistance line of the pattern which is separating the two lows, you should enter a long position in the security as it indicates a bullish reversal in the security.

Profit Target: The profit target for this pattern should match the distance between the lowest point in the pattern and its resistance neckline level. When the price matches the calculated distance, one can book profits from the trade. Otherwise, you can also target profits till the next immediate resistance level.

Stop Loss: The resistance line of the chart pattern should be the trigger for stop-loss while trading using this pattern. One should place a stop loss a few points below the resistance line of the pattern.

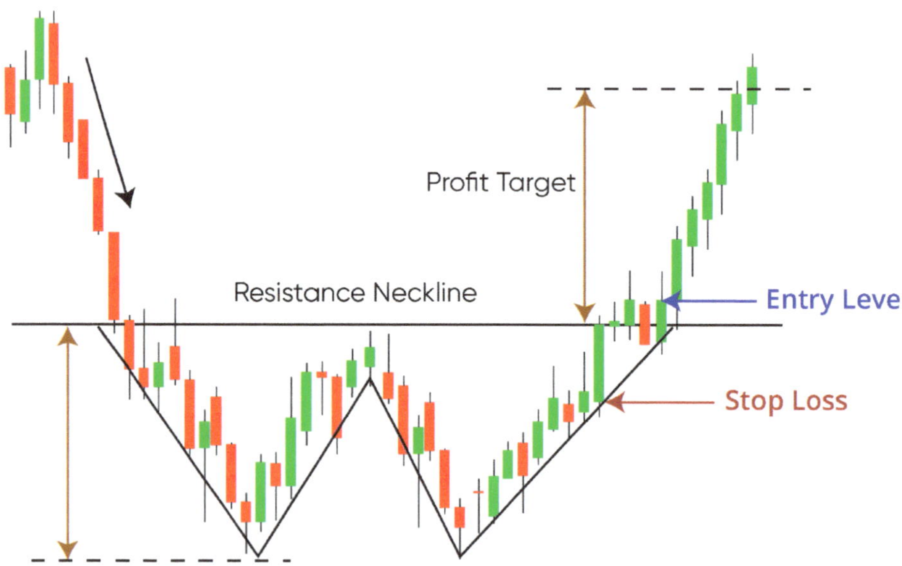

Fig. Double Bottom Pattern

7) Flag and Pole Pattern

A flag and pole pattern is a bullish continuation pattern formed when there is a sharp upward move in the price of security followed by consolidation within a small range. The consolidation is again likely followed by a strong uptrend in the market.

How to trade using the Flag and Pole pattern?

Entry: When the price of the security breaks above the consolidated upper trendline price which has formed a flag pattern, you can enter a long position in the security, as the breakout indicates the continuation of the existing trend.

Profit Target: The profit target for this pattern should match the height of the pole pattern that is formed before the small consolidation. When the price matches the calculated distance after the breakout, one can book profits from the trade. Else, you can also target profits till the next immediate resistance level in the chart.

Stop Loss: When the price of the security moves a few points below the consolidated flag pattern, one should exit the trade from the security.

Fig. Flag and Pole Pattern

8) Inverted Flag and Pole Pattern

This pattern works opposite of the Flag and pole pattern discussed earlier. An Inverted flag and pole pattern is a bearish continuation pattern formed when there is a sharp downward move in the price of security followed by consolidation within a small range. The consolidation is again likely followed by a strong downtrend in the market.

How to trade using the Inverted Flag and Pole pattern?

Entry Level: When the price of the security breaks below the consolidated price, which has formed a flag pattern, you can enter a short position in the security, as the breakdown indicates the continuation of the existing trend.

Profit Target: The profit target for this pattern should match the height of the pole pattern that is formed before the small consolidation. When the price matches the calculated distance after the breakout, one can book profits from the trade. Otherwise, you can also target profits till the next immediate support level in the chart.

Stop Loss: When the price of the security moves a few points above the consolidated flag pattern, one should exit the trade from the security.

Fig. Inverted Flag & Pole Pattern

9) Head and Shoulder Pattern

A head and shoulder pattern is a bearish reversal pattern that is formed when the price of the security forms three peaks that are separated by a pullback, which forms the neckline for the pattern.

The middle peak formed in this pattern is the highest compared to the peaks beside it. This pattern indicates that the buyers have been exhausted after trying to push the price up and are overpowered by sellers in the market. When the price breaks below the neckline of the pattern, it is an indication of a bearish reversal in the market.

How to trade using the Head and Shoulder Pattern?

Entry Level: When the price of the security breaks below the neckline of the pattern that separates the three peaks, you should enter a short position in the security as it indicates a bearish reversal in the security.

Profit Target: The profit target for this pattern should match the distance between the highest point in the pattern and its neckline. When the price matches the calculated distance, one can book profits from the trade.

Stop Loss: The neckline of the chart pattern should be the trigger for stop-loss while trading using this pattern. One should place a stop loss a few points above the support neckline of the pattern.

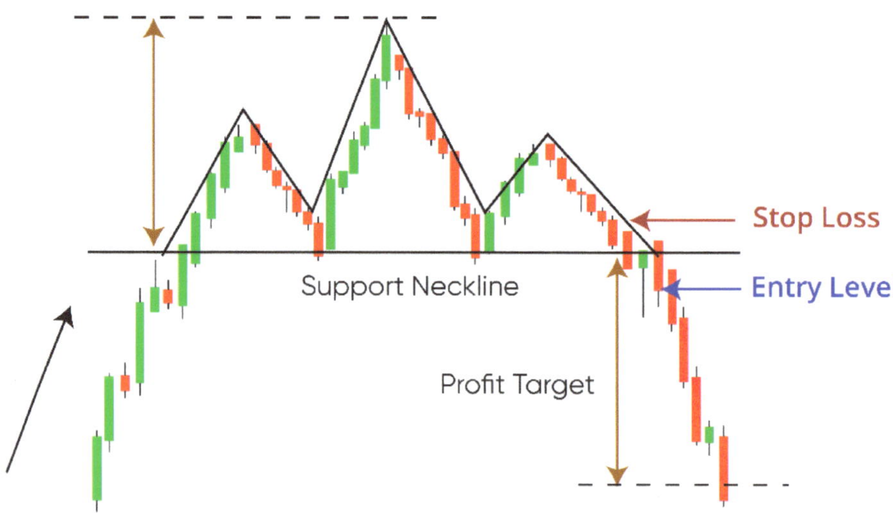

Fig. Head and Shoulder Pattern

10) Inverted Head and Shoulder Pattern

The Inverted Head and Shoulder Pattern is the reverse of the Head and Shoulder pattern discussed earlier. An Inverted head and shoulder pattern is a bullish reversal pattern that is formed when the price of the security forms three lows that are separated by a pullback, which forms the neckline for the pattern.

The centre low formed in this pattern is the lowest compared to the other two lows made beside it. This pattern indicates that the sellers have been exhausted after trying to push the price down and are overpowered by buyers in the market. When the price breaks above the neckline of the pattern, it is an indication of a bullish reversal in the market.

How to trade an Inverted Head and Shoulder Pattern?

Entry: When the price of the security breaks above the resistance neckline of the pattern that separates the three lows, you should enter a long position in the security as it indicates a bullish reversal in the security.

Profit Target: The profit target for this pattern should match the distance between the lowest point in the pattern and its neckline. When the price matches the calculated distance, one can book profits from the trade.

Stop Loss: The neckline of the chart pattern should be the trigger for stop-loss while trading using this pattern. One should place a stop loss a few points below the neckline of the pattern.

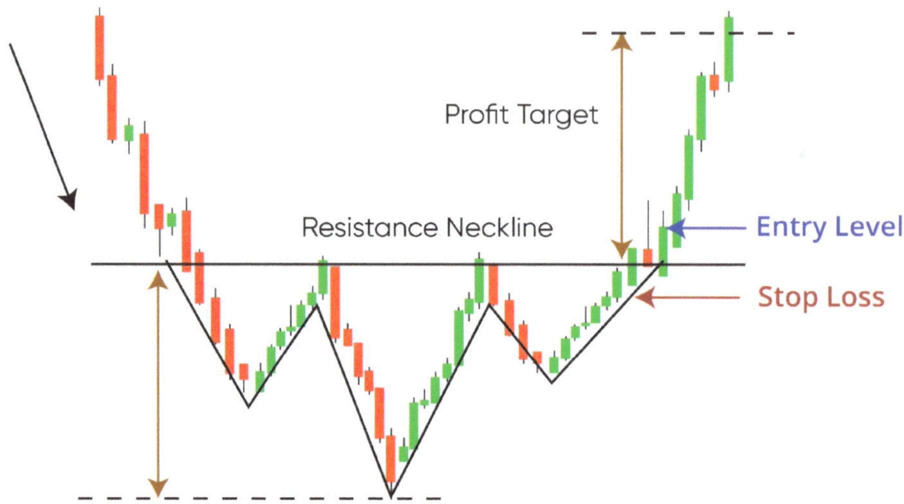

Fig. Inverted Head and Shoulder Pattern

11) Rounding Bottom Pattern

A Rounding Bottom pattern is a bullish reversal pattern that is formed when the price declines to a low after a downtrend and consolidates within a narrow range before rising upwards.

This movement in price movement makes a 'U' shape, which indicates that the selling pressure is weakening and the buyers are taking control of the market which leads to a gradual price increase. In order to trade the rounding bottom pattern, you need to draw a resistance line (neckline) at the swing highs of the pattern and wait for the price to break above the neckline.

How to trade using the Rounding Bottom Pattern?

Entry Level: When the price of the security breaks above the resistance neckline of the pattern, one can enter a long position in the security as it indicates a reversal on the upside.

Profit Target: The profit target for this pattern should match the distance between the lowest point in the pattern and its neckline. When the price matches the calculated distance, one can book profits from the trade.

Stop Loss: The neckline of the chart pattern should be the trigger for stop-loss while trading using this pattern. One should place a stop loss a few points below the neckline of the pattern.

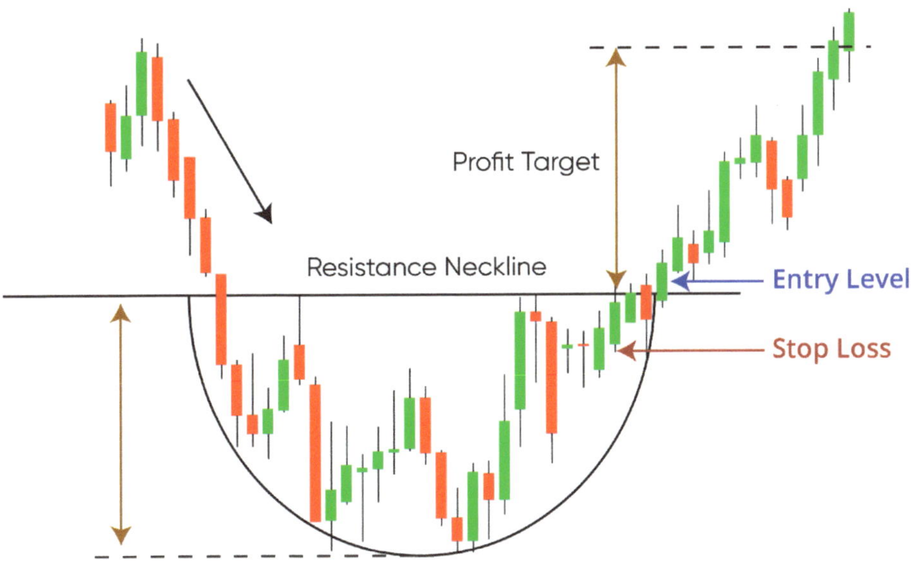

Fig. Rounding Bottom Pattern

12) Rounding Top Pattern

A Rounding Bottom pattern is a bearish reversal pattern that is formed when the price rises to a high after an uptrend and consolidates within a narrow range before fall downwards.

This movement in price movement makes an inverted 'U' shape which indicates that the buying pressure is weakening and the sellers are taking control of the market which leads to a gradual price decrease. In order to trade the rounding Top pattern, you need to draw a support line (neckline) at the swing low of the pattern and wait for the price to break below the neckline.

How to trade using the Rounding Top Pattern?

Entry Level: When the price of the security breaks below the neckline of the pattern, enter a short position in the security as it indicates a reversal on the downside.

Profit Target: The profit target for this pattern should match the distance between the highest point in the pattern and its neckline. When the price matches the calculated distance, one can book profits from the trade.

Stop Loss: The neckline of the chart pattern should be the trigger for stop-loss while trading using this pattern. One should place a stop loss a few points above the neckline of the pattern.

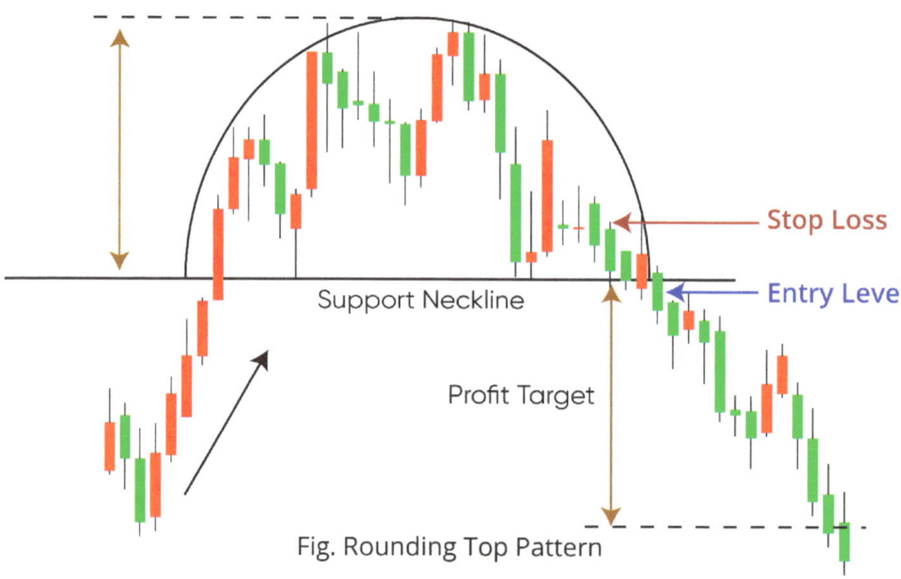

Fig. Rounding Top Pattern

13) Cup and Handle Pattern

The cup and handle pattern is a bullish continuation pattern that resembles the shape of a teacup. This pattern typically forms after an uptrend and comprises a period of consolidation that looks like the shape of a cup. As the security rises upwards, a small pullback occurs, forming the handle portion of the pattern. The handle is a short consolidation period whose height is one-third height of the cup.

In order to trade the Cup and Handle Pattern, you need to draw a resistance line (neckline) at the swing highs of the pattern and wait for the price to break above the neckline.

How to trade using the Cup and Handle Pattern?

Entry Level: When the price of the security breaks above the neckline of the pattern enter a long position in the security as it indicates a resumption in the bullish trend.

Profit Target: The profit target for this pattern should match the distance between the lowest point in the pattern and its neckline. When the price matches the calculated distance, one can book profits from the trade.

Stop Loss: The lowest point of the handle in the chart pattern should be the trigger for stop-loss while trading using this pattern. A stop-loss should be placed below the low point of the handle.

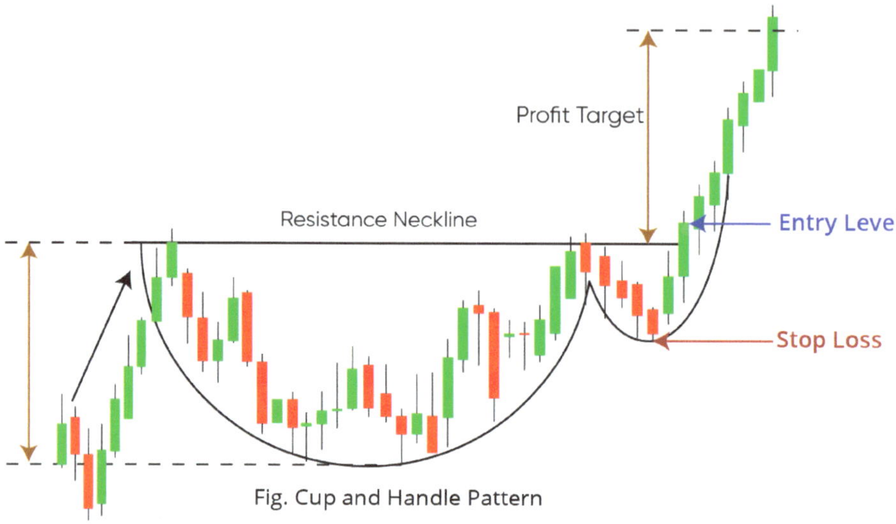

Fig. Cup and Handle Pattern

14) Inverted Cup and Handle Pattern

The Inverted cup and handle pattern is a bearish continuation pattern that resembles the shape of an upside-down teacup. This pattern typically forms after a downtrend and comprises a period of consolidation that looks like the shape of an inverted cup. As the security price declines, a small pullback occurs, forming the handle portion of the pattern. The handle is a short consolidation period whose height is one-third height of the cup.

In order to trade the inverted Cup and Handle Pattern, you need to draw a support line (neckline) at the swing lows of the pattern and wait for the price to break below the neckline.

How to Trade using the inverted Cup and Handle Pattern?

Entry: When the price of the security breaks below the neckline of the pattern enter a short position in the security as it indicates resumption in the bearish trend.

Profit Target: The profit target for this pattern should match the distance between the highest point in the pattern and its neckline. When the price matches the calculated distance, one can book profits from the trade.

Stop Loss: The highest point of the handle in the chart pattern should be the trigger for stop-loss while trading using this pattern. A stoploss should be placed above the high point of handle.

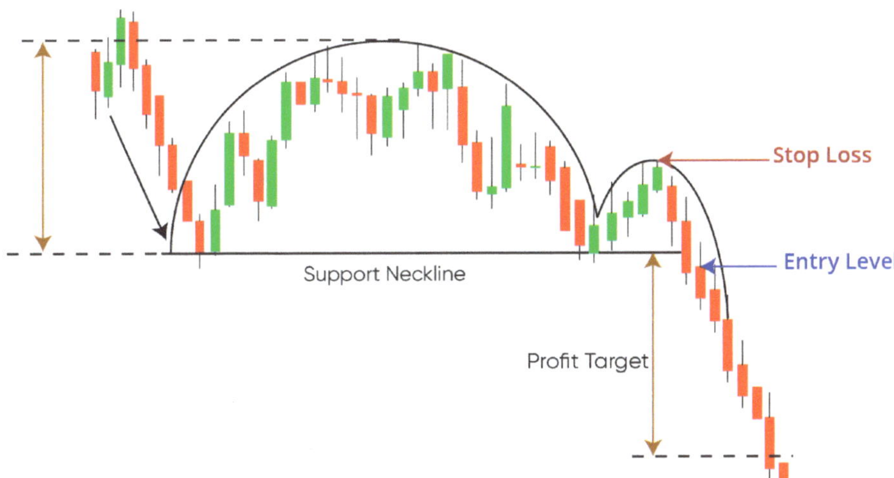

Fig. Inverted Cup and handle Pattern

15) Diamond Bottom Pattern

The Diamond Bottom Pattern is a bullish reversal pattern formed when the price of the security makes a series of increasing ranges of swings followed by a decreasing range of swings. The highs and lows from the price swings form the shape of a diamond when connected using trendlines. This pattern signals a shift from bearish to bullish sentiments at the bottom of the downtrend.

How to trade using the Diamond Bottom Pattern?

Entry: When the price breaks above the upper trendline of the pattern, you can enter a long position in the security as it indicates a bullish reversal in the security.

Profit Target: The profit target for this pattern should match the distance between the lowest point in the pattern and the highest point in the pattern. When the price matches the calculated distance, one can book profits from the trade.

Stop Loss: The stop loss for this pattern should be placed below the recent swing low of the pattern.

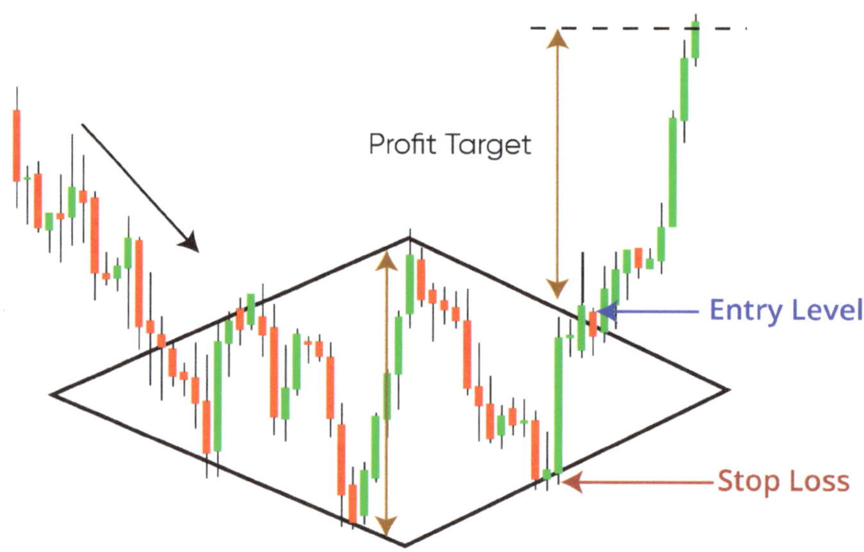

Fig. Diamond Bottom Pattern

16) Diamond Top Pattern

The Diamond Top Pattern is a twin of the diamond bottom pattern, and it indicates a bearish reversal after an uptrend. This pattern also comprises a series of increasing ranges of swings followed by a decreasing range of swings. The highs and lows from the price swings form the shape of a diamond when connected using trendlines. This pattern signals a shift from bullish to bearish sentiments at the top of the uptrend.

How to trade using the Diamond Top Pattern?

Entry: When the price breaks below the lower trendline of the pattern, you can enter a short position in the security as it indicates a bearish reversal in the security.

Profit Target: The profit target for this pattern should match the distance between the highest point in the pattern and the lowest point in the pattern. When the price matches the calculated distance, one can book profits from the trade.

Stop Loss: The stop loss for this pattern should be placed above the recent swing high of the pattern.

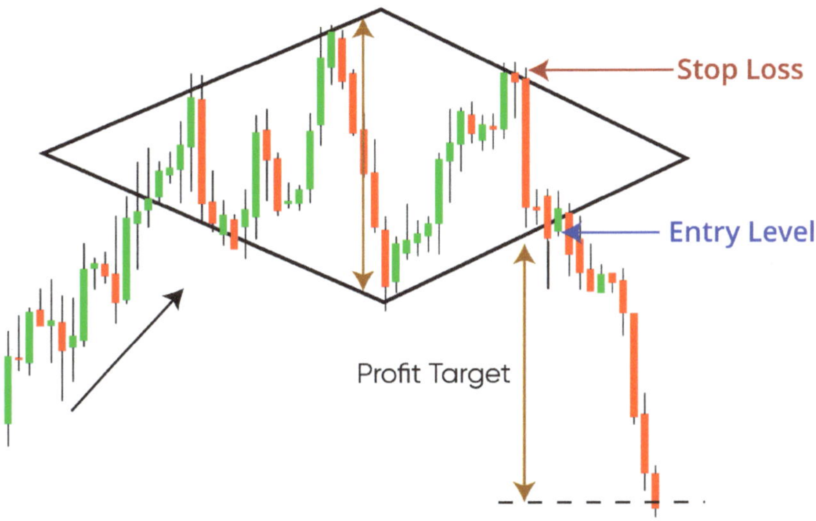

Fig. Diamond Top Pattern

17) Broadening Bottom Pattern

The broadening bottom is a bullish reversal pattern found at the bottom of the downtrend. This chart pattern looks like a megaphone. It comprises two diverging trendlines formed by a series of increasing swing highs and lows in security. The increase in the volatility in the pattern indicates a potential breakout to the upside in the security.

How to trade using the Broadening Bottom Pattern?

Entry: When the price breaks above the upper trendline of the pattern, you can enter a long position in the security.

Profit Target: The profit target for this pattern should match the distance between the lowest and the highest point in the pattern. When the price matches the calculated distance, one can book profits from the trade.

Stop Loss: The stop loss for this pattern should be placed a few points below the upper trendline of the pattern

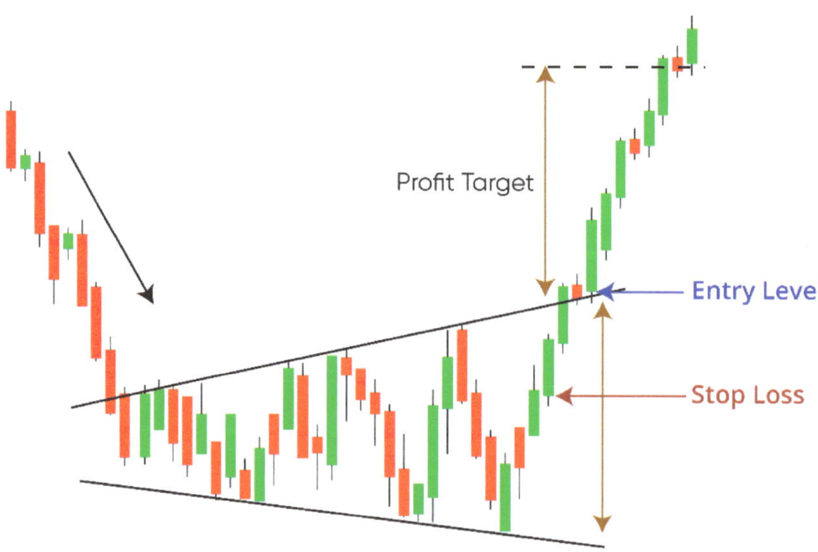

Fig. Broadening Bottom Pattern

18) Broadening Top Pattern

The broadening Top is a bearish reversal pattern found at the top of the uptrend. This has a similar composition of a broadening bottom pattern. It comprises two diverging trendlines formed by a series of increasing swing highs and lows in security. The increase in the volatility in the pattern after an uptrend indicates a potential breakout to the downside in the security.

How to trade using the Broadening Top Pattern?

Entry: When the price breaks below the lower trendline of the pattern, you can enter a short position in the security.

Profit Target: The profit target for this pattern should match the distance between the lowest and the highest point in the pattern. When the price matches the calculated distance, one can book profits from the trade.

Stop Loss: The stop loss for this pattern should be placed a few points above the lower trendline of the pattern.

Fig. Broadening Top Pattern

19) Descending Broadening Wedge Pattern

The Descending Broadening wedge pattern is a bullish reversal pattern that comprises two downward-sloping trendlines that diverge from each other. Here, the security is moving downwards, making lower highs and comparatively more aggressive lower lows. This pattern indicates a potential bullish reversal after a period of increased volatility.

How to trade using the Descending Broadening wedge pattern?

Entry: When the price breaks above the upper trendline of the pattern, you can enter a long position in the security.

Profit Target: The profit target for this pattern should match the distance between the lowest and the highest point in the pattern. When the price matches the calculated distance, one can book profits from the trade.

Stop Loss: The stop loss for this pattern should be placed a few points below the upper trendline of the pattern

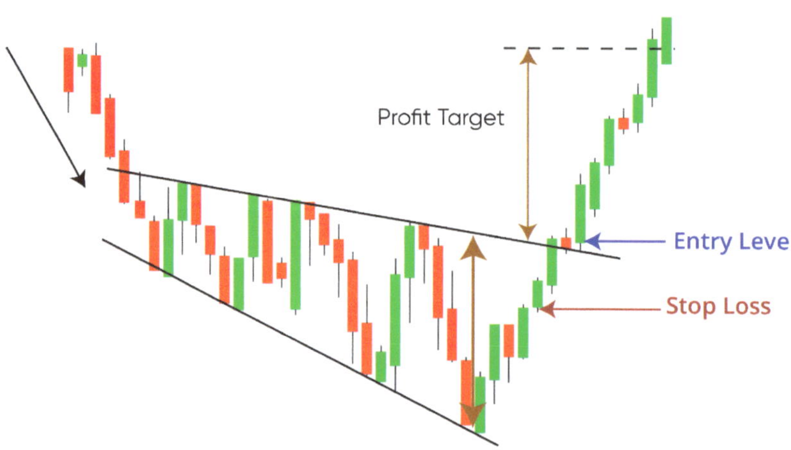

Fig. Descending Broadening Wedge Pattern

20) Ascending Broadening Wedge Pattern

The Ascending Broadening wedge pattern is a bearish reversal pattern that comprises two upward-sloping trendlines that diverge from each other. Here, the security is moving upwards, making higher lows and comparatively more aggressive higher highs. This pattern indicates a potential bearish reversal after a period of increased volatility.

How to trade using the Descending Broadening wedge pattern?

Entry: When the price breaks below the lower trendline of the pattern, you can enter a short position in the security.

Profit Target: The profit target for this pattern should match the distance between the highest and the lowest point in the pattern. When the price matches the calculated distance, one can book profits from the trade.

Stop Loss: The stop loss for this pattern should be placed a few points above the lower trendline of the pattern

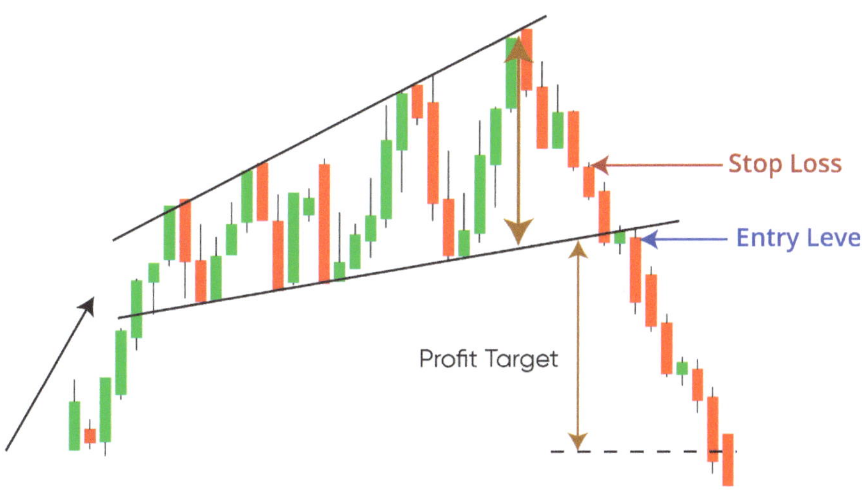

Fig. Ascending Broadening Wedge Pattern

21) Symmetrical Triangle Pattern

The Symmetrical triangle pattern is a continuation pattern that can be used for bullish or bearish continuation. This pattern is formed when the price is consolidating which causes the trendlines to converge with each other. Here, the upper trendline and the lower trendline have roughly equal slopes which makes the look symmetrical. This pattern indicates an indecision between the buyers and sellers in the market.

While this pattern is known to be used for confirmation, it can also be used for reversals after a significant uptrend or downtrend.

How to trade using the Symmetrical triangle pattern?

Entry Level: If the price of the security breaks above the upper trendline of the chart pattern, one can enter a long position in the security. Similarly, if the price breaks below the lower trendline of the pattern, you can enter a short position in the security.

Profit Target: The profit target for this pattern should match the distance between the lowest and the highest point in the pattern. When the price matches the calculated distance after the break, one can book profits from the trade.

Stop Loss: If a long position has been entered, place a stop loss a few points below the entry. Similarly, for a short position, place your stop loss a few points above the point of entry.

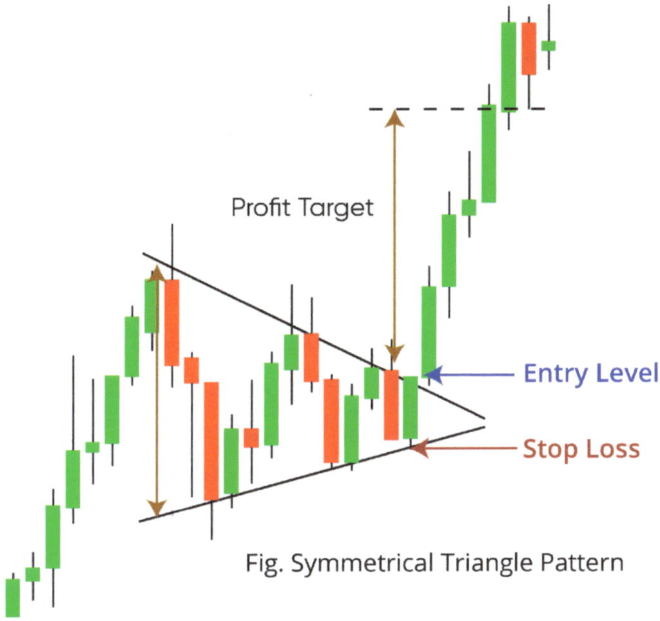

Fig. Symmetrical Triangle Pattern

The above chart shows Symmetrical Trading pattern during an uptrend. And the below chart shows trading Symmetrical Trading pattern during a downtrend.

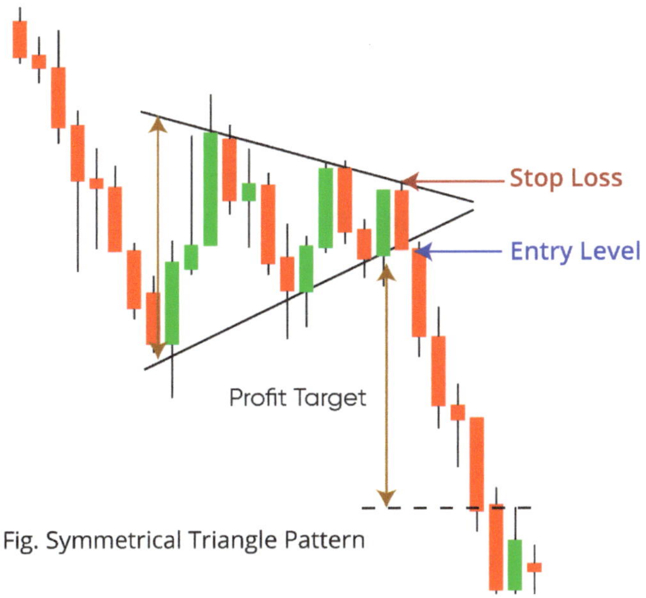

Fig. Symmetrical Triangle Pattern

TECHNICAL INDICATORS

Till now, we have discussed multiple charts and patterns that are used by the Traders to identify trades. In this chapter, we will discuss the next most important tool that most traders massively rely upon to confirm their entry and exit while making trades, and it is known as Technical Indicators.

Technical indicators are generally tools that are used in technical analysis and help in indicating where the price will go next using mathematical calculations. A few of the popular technical indicators used by traders are the Moving Average, RSI, Fibonacci retracement, MACD, etc.

In general, we can classify Technical indicators into five categories based on how and where they are used:

1. Trend Indicator– These particular indicators indicate the trend of the market or the direction in which the market is moving. Examples: SMA, EMA, MACD etc
2. Support and resistance indicators- These indicators work as support and resistance channels in charts. For example, EMA, Pivot Points, Fibonacci levels, etc.
3. Momentum Indicator – These indicators indicate the strength of the trend in the market and whether there will be a reversal in the market. For example: RSI, ADX, CCI etc

4. Volume Indicator – Volume indicators indicate the change in volume with time. It also indicates the number of stocks being bought and sold over time. For example: VWAP, On-Balance Volume (OBV), Volume Profile Indicator etc.
5. Volatility Indicator– It indicates how much the price is changing in a given period and gives an indication of how much the price is changing in the present. For example, Bollinger Bands, ATR, Keltner Channel etc.

In addition, the technical indicators can also be classified into leading and lagging indicators. There are certain indicators that try to pre-empt the likely move in the market. They use different ingredients and try to understand what could be the likely move in the prices of the underlying asset. These indicators are called Leading Indicators. For example, RSI, CCI, Stochastic Indicator, Fibonacci retracement, Pivot Points are examples of leading indicators.

On the other hand, there are certain indicators that try to understand the historical price movement and do a post mortem analysis. These are called Lagging Indicators. For example, EMA, SMA, Supertrend, Bollinger Bands etc are the examples of lagging indicators.

There are thousands of technical indicators available for traders. However, for the scope of this book, we are going to cover only five of the most important and commonly used technical indicators that every trader should know.

1) Moving Average (MA)

Moving averages are a technical indicator calculated as an average of the past closing price of the security over a specific period. These averages are plotted along the price of the security and help us identify the trends in the prices.

The moving average indicator can be calculated for any chosen period, such as 5 period, 9 period, 50 period, 200 period, etc, based on short-term and long-term trading strategies.

Depending on the basis of its calculation, moving averages can be broadly categorized into three categories, i.e, the simple moving average (SMA), the exponential moving average (EMA) and the weighted moving average (WMA). Let us understand the difference between of these types of moving averages.

- **Simple Moving Average:** It is calculated by averaging the closing prices of the security over a given period. The average is considered by giving equal weightage to all the closing prices. As new closing prices are added, the oldest prices are dropped, creating a new moving average.
- **Exponential Moving Average:** EMA is a type of moving average that assigns more weight to the recent price points on the chart. Here, the weights assigned to the closing prices will increase exponentially.

Note: While the simple moving average assigns equal weight to all the prices, the exponential moving average assigns more weight to recent data which allows it to react quickly to new trends in the market.

- **Weighted Moving Average:** Similar to the Exponential moving average, the weighted moving average also assigns more weight to the recent price points on the chart. Here, the weights assigned to the closing prices increase linearly.

In general, SMAs and EMAs are more frequently used by traders as moving average indicators compared to WMAs.

Exponential Moving Average

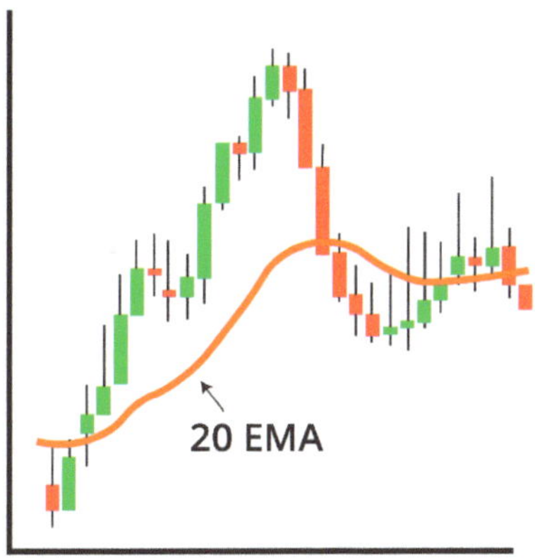

Pros:

- Assigns more weightage to recent price data which helps in faster identification of the trends.
- Reduces Lag compared to SMA making it more suitable for short term trading

Cons:

- More susceptible to false signals during volatile markets due to its responsiveness to recent price changes

Simple Moving Average

Pros:

- Smoothened price data over a specified period, which makes it easier to identify the trend.
- Less sensitive to short-term price fluctuations which reduces the false signals

Cons:

- Does not react quickly to recent price changes as it assigns equal weights to all price data within the period

Application of Moving Averages

Moving averages can be used in multiple ways by traders. Below are some of the ways in which moving averages can be utilized:

1) Trend Identification

Moving averages help us understand the overall direction in the price of the security on the basis of the price move above or below the moving average. This is one of the most prominent features of the moving indicator.

The way the moving average indicator helps in trend identification is rather straightforward. When the price moves above a moving average, it is considered that the security is in an uptrend and one can consider entering a long position in the security by placing a stop-loss a few points below the entry level.

Similarly, when the price moves below a moving average, it is considered that the security is in a downtrend and one can consider entering a short position in the security by placing a stop-loss a few points above the entry level.

Here, the bigger or long-term moving averages give fewer signals but they tend to be more accurate. On the other hand, the short-term moving averages tend to give many signals but their accuracy tends to decrease.

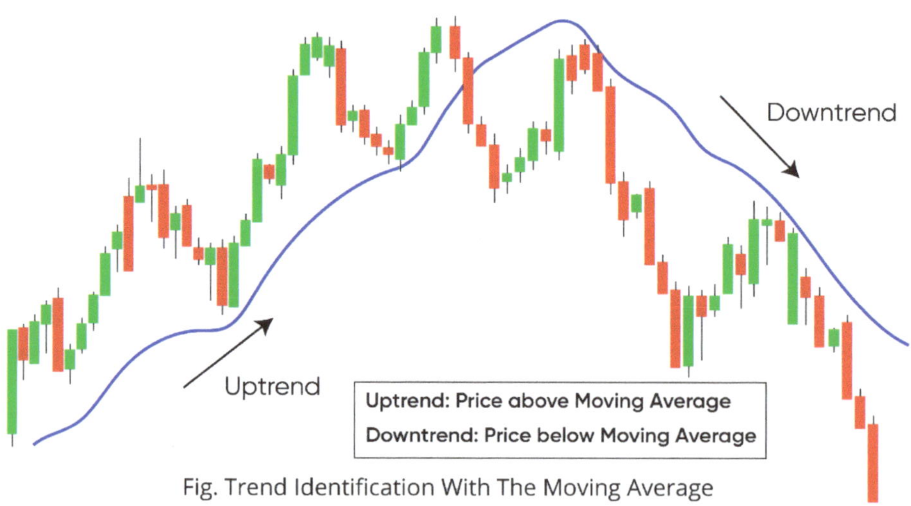

Fig. Trend Identification With The Moving Average

2) Support and Resistance:-

Another handy and alternative use of moving average is using it as a dynamic support and resistance level.

When the price is trading above moving average it tends to act as a support level from where the security tends to reverse upwards. If the price breaks below the moving average line, it is recommended to close any long positions open in the security.

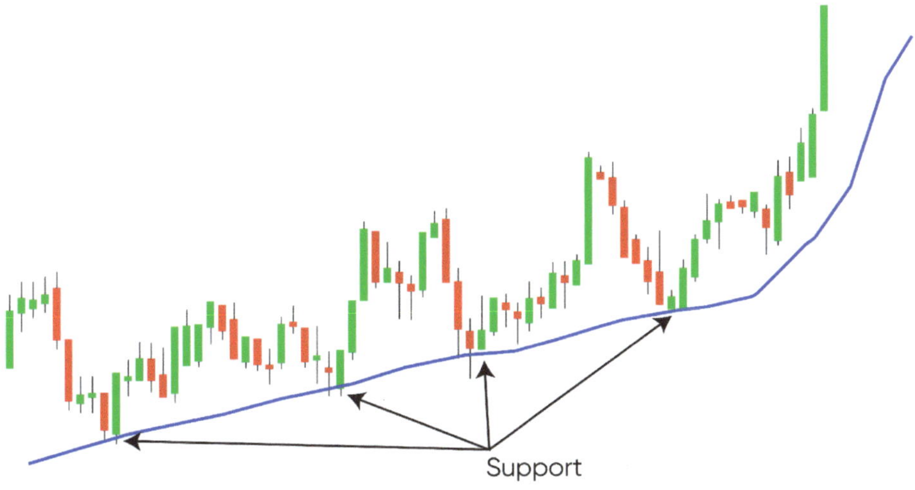

Fig. Moving Average Acting As Support

Similarly, if the price is trading below a moving average it tends to act as a resistance level from where the security tends to reverse downwards. If the price breaks above the moving average line, it is recommended to close any short positions open in the security

Fig. Moving Average Acting As Resistance

It's important to note that when using the moving average as a support or resistance, one should use larger timeframes rather than smaller ones. This is because long-term moving averages fluctuate less in response to price changes compared to short-term moving averages. For example, 50 EMA, 100 EMA, 200 EMA can act as good support and resistance levels.

Moving Average Crossover Strategy

A moving average crossover is a strategy that uses more than one moving average in order to identify the entry and exit levels in the security. Here, the moving averages used should be a combination of two different moving averages, ideally a short-term moving average and a long-term moving average.

Here is how this moving averages crossover strategy works:

1) For Long Position

When a short-term moving average crosses above the long-term moving average, it indicates a shift to bullish momentum in the security.

Here, one can enter a long position when a green candle closes above both the moving averages and the price starts trading above it. The stop-loss for this trade should be placed a few points below the entry-level.

The profits for this trade can be booked by trailing the moving average until the shorter MA crosses below the longer MA or when the price breaks below any one of the moving averages.

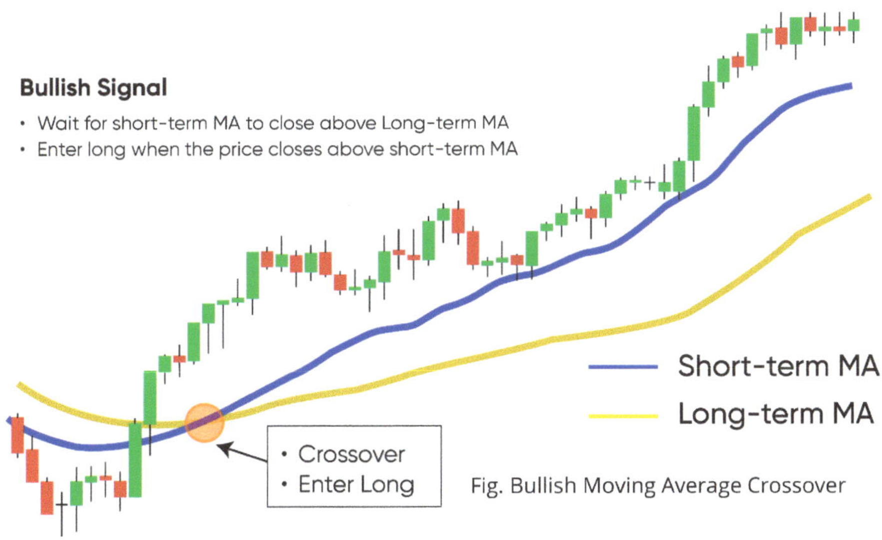

Fig. Bullish Moving Average Crossover

2) For Short Position

When a short-term moving average crosses below the long-term moving average, it indicates a shift to bearish momentum in the security. Here, one can enter a short position when a red candle closes below both the moving averages and the price starts trading below it. The stop-loss for this trade should be placed a few points above the entry-level.

The profits for this trade can be booked by trailing the moving average until the shorter MA crosses above the longer MA or when the price breaks above any one of the moving averages.

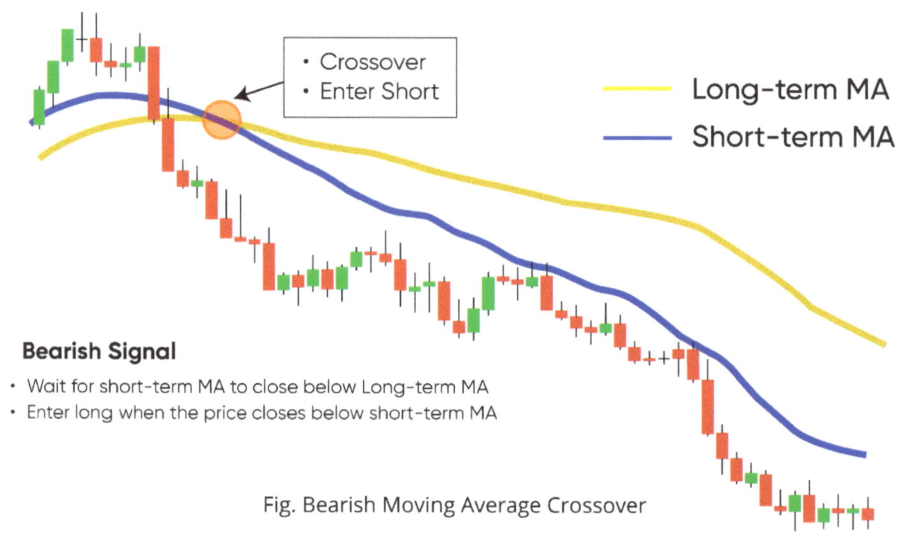

Fig. Bearish Moving Average Crossover

Combination of different Moving Averages

The combination of moving average crossovers differs for different timeframes. For instance, for shorter timeframes like intraday trading, the popular moving average combinations include 5-9 moving averages and 5-8-13 moving averages.

On larger time frames like positional and swing trading, the popular moving average combination is the 50-200 moving average which is also referred to as golden and death cross strategy.

2) Relative Strength Index (RSI)

The Relative Strength Index (RSI) is a leading indicator developed by J. Welles Wilder and used in market analysis. It is a momentum oscillator which measures the speed and change of price movements.

This indicator oscillates between a range of 0 to 100 in which the range can be adjusted according to the strategies. Generally, the default setting for the RSI is 14 days, which means the RSI zone is derived by considering the average of gains and losses over a period of 14 days.

RSI indicator is mainly used to identify the over-bought and over-sold zones in the market. When the RSI is below the range of 30, it means that the security is in the oversold zone and it is considered that the security is in a favourable buying condition.

Fig. RSI Indicating Oversold Zone

When the RSI is trading above the range of 70, it means that the RSI is in the overbought zone and it is considered that the security is in a favourable selling condition.

Fig. RSI Indicating Overbrought Zone

While the RSI tells if a security is in an oversold or overbought zone, it is difficult to determine to exact point of entering a trade using this indicator. Therefore, it is best to RSI indicator as additional confirmation for an already existing trade setup like the candlesticks, chart patterns and support & resistance levels.

RSI Divergence

RSI Divergence is a strategy that indicates a strong potential price reversal in the security. This occurs when the price of the securities direction is opposite to the change in momentum of the RSI indicator. The Divergences can be categorized into bullish and bearish divergences and here's how you can identify each of these divergences.

Bullish Divergence

A bullish divergence is formed when the price of the security is making a lower low but the RSI indicator is diverging by making higher lows. This indicates a rising bullish momentum and one can enter a long position once an additional confirmation for the bullish reversal is obtained.

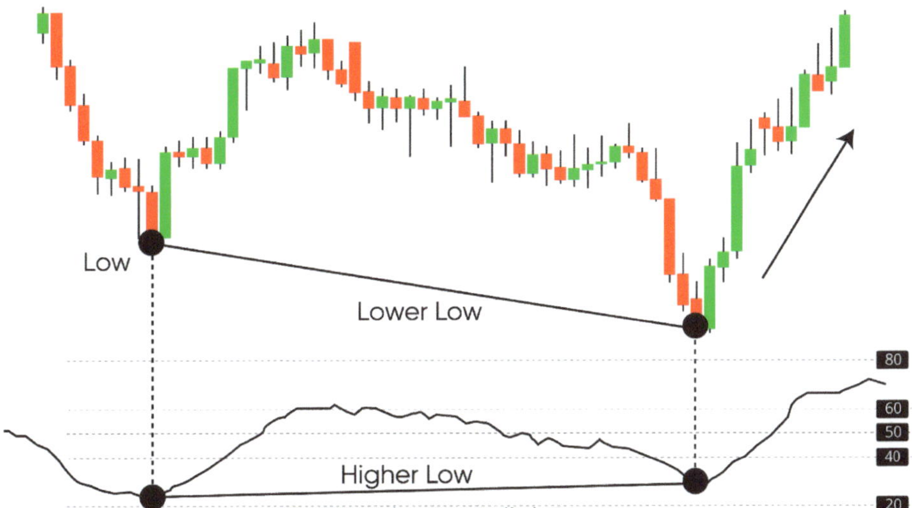

Fig. RSI Indicating Bullish Divergence

Bearish Divergence

A bearish divergence is formed when the price of the security is making higher highs but the RSI indicator is diverging by making lower highs. This indicates an increasing bearish momentum and one can enter a short position once an additional confirmation for the bearish reversal is obtained.

Fig. RSI Indicating Bearish Divergence

3) Fibonacci Sequence

Developed by Leonardo Fibonacci in the 13th century, the Fibonacci sequence is a series of numbers starting with zero and one which gradually increases with each number equal to the sum of the two numbers before it.

Therefore, the sequence will be as follows: 0, 1, 1, 2, 3, 5, 8, 13, 21, 34, 55, 89, 144, 233, 377, 610 and so on, which will extend to infinity. Here, each number is approximately 1.618 times greater than its previous number. The value 1.618 is also referred to as the golden ratio.

The value 1.6818 is referred to as the 'Golden Ratio" or Phi. This value is derived by selecting any number in the Fibonacci sequence and dividing it by the number before it.

This value often mysteriously appears in the natural world, fine art, architecture and biology. For instance, this ratio has been noticed in the painting of Mona Lisa, in sunflowers, tree branches, human faces, rose petals and even the spiral galaxies of outer space. This ratio can also be extensively used in Fibonacci Trading

What are Retracements?

Retracements are movements in the opposite direction of the stock price's existing movement. These are temporary movements and do not indicate the wider trend in the market.

What are Fibonacci Retracement Levels?

Fibonacci retracement levels, derived from the Fibonacci sequence, are horizontal lines that indicate where support and resistance are expected to occur. These levels will appear using the Fibonacci retracement tool by connecting the highest and the lowest point in the security

Each level is represented by a percentage. The percentage represents the measurement of the price correction or pullback in relation to the prior trend.

The Fibonacci levels of retracement are 23.6%, 38.2%, 61.8%, and 78.6%. While not an official Fibonacci ratio, 50% is also used as a level of Fibonacci retracement.

These levels are useful as they can help us identify the level where a security might resume to move in its initial trend.

How To Use Fibonacci Retracement

Fibonacci Retracement can be used by traders to draw support levels, identify resistance levels, place stop-loss orders, and set target prices. Let us now understand how to use Fibonacci Retracement in an uptrend and a downtrend.

How to use Fibonacci Retracement in an Uptrend?

Fibonacci retracement tool is generally available in most of the charting platforms and websites. Following are the steps to be followed to use Fibonacci retracement in an Uptrend:

1. Identify the Uptrend:

When the price of the security is making higher high for a significant duration, you can use the Fibonacci retracement tool, as the security tends to retrace during any trend.

2. Apply Fibonacci Retracement Levels:

When the price of the security retraces from an uptrend, connect the low point and the high point of the security using the Fibonacci retracement tool. This will give you the different levels of Fibonacci retracement.

3. Entry Point:

When the price of the security retraces to one of the Fibonacci levels, one can consider entering a long position in the security. Traders may look for additional confirmation signals, such as candlestick patterns or indicators, to confirm the entry.

4. Profit Target

One can consider booking profits from the trade when the price of the security reaches the high point from where the price had retraced.

5. Stop Loss

One can place a stop-loss a few points below the Fibonacci level from where the trade has been entered.

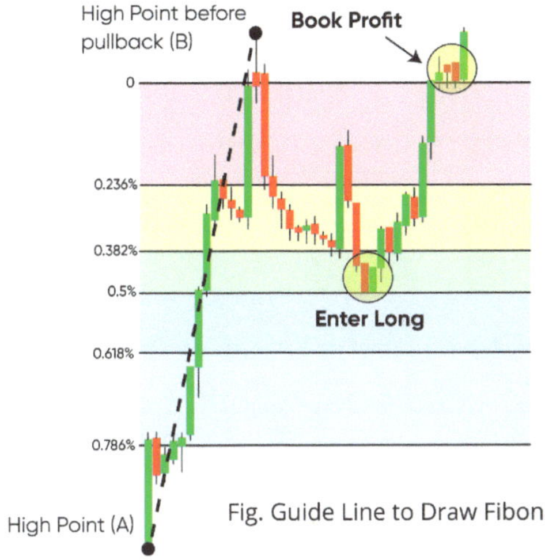

Steps:

1. Start the fibonacci point from the high point (A) of the Uptrend.
2. End the fibonacci point at the high point before the pullback (B).
3. Enter Long when the price retraces from a fibonacci level.
4. Place a stop loss few points below entry.
5. Book profits near the previous high

Fig. Guide Line to Draw Fibonacci Levels in Uptrend

How to use Fibonacci Retracement in a Downtrend?

Following are the steps to be followed to use Fibonacci retracement in a Downtrend:

1. Identify the Downtrend:

When the price of the security is making lower lows for a significant duration, you can use the Fibonacci retracement tool, as the security tends to retrace during any trend.

2. Apply Fibonacci Retracement Levels:

When the price of the security retraces from the downtrend, identify the high and the low price to the point of its retracement. Connect the high point and the low point of the security using the Fibonacci retracement tool. This will give you the different levels of Fibonacci retracement.

3. Entry Point:

When the price of the security retraces to one of the Fibonacci levels, one can consider entering a short position in the security. Just like in the uptrend, traders can look for additional confirmation signals to confirm the entry.

4. Profit Target

One can consider booking profits from the trade when the price of the security reaches the low point from where the price had retraced.

5. Stop Loss

One can place a stop-loss a few points above the Fibonacci level from where the trade has been entered.

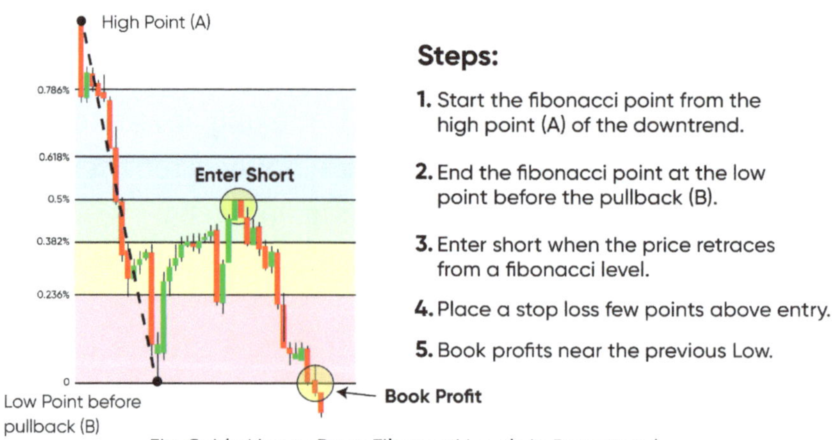

Fig. Guide Line to Draw Fibonacci Levels in Downtrend

How much should a security retrace?

If the security retraces up to 50% on the Fibonacci scale after a significant uptrend or a downtrend, it is considered that the primary trend is still intact, and the price will likely reverse in that direction

A security retracing up to 61.8% on the fibonacci scale indicates that the primary is weakening and the price may likely move against it.

4) Bollinger Bands

Bollinger Bands, developed by John Bollinger in the 1980s, is a technical analysis tool defined by a set of three lines to generate overbought and oversold zones of the securities.

The three lines of the Bollinger Bands are a simple moving average or middle band, upper band and lower band. The Upper and lower bands comprise standard deviations from a 20-day simple moving average.

Bollinger Bands are placed over a price chart, it is also a volatility indicator which depicts quick trend reversals in the securities.

Trading strategies with Bollinger Bands

The following are the strategies involved with Bollinger Bands to generate better trading opportunities.

Overbought and Oversold Zone

Market participants generally use Bollinger Bands to identify overbought and oversold zones.

Overbought Zone

When the price of the security moves above the upper band it is considered as a overbought zone. A long position can be closed when the price of the security is above the upper band. Also, at the same point, a new entry for the short position can be spotted.

Oversold Zone

As the price of the security lowers below the lower band it is considered an oversold zone. Here, the short position placed can be closed. In the oversold zone, a fresh opportunity for entry into the long position will be spotted.

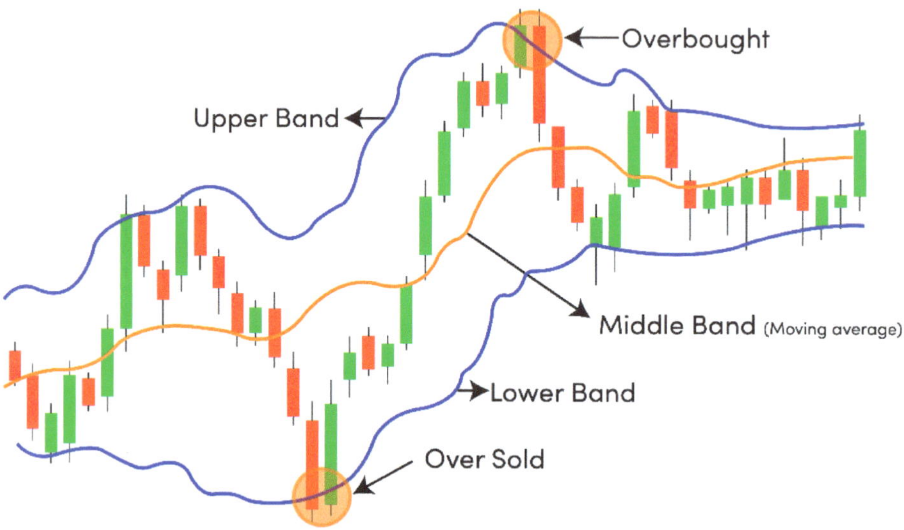

Fig. Bollinger Band Components And Overbought/Sold Zones

Volatility

Bollinger Bands can be used as a volatility indicator to measure the volatility. When the bands contract, it signifies low volatility of the security. In the time frame with high volatility, the bands expand. The below chart shows how the band contracted when the security was moving sideways i.e., during a low volatility and how it expanded during a fast uptrend after increased volatility.

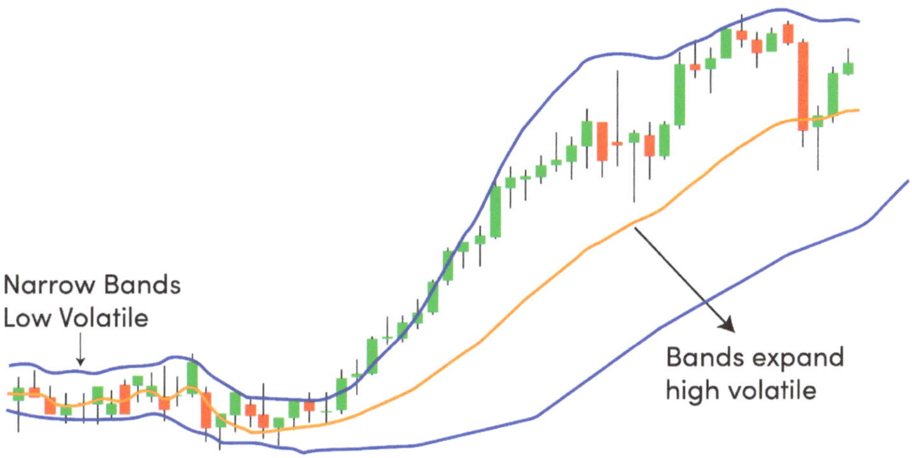

Fig. Bollinger Band As Volatily Indicators

Trends with Bollinger Bands

The middle band of Bollinger Bands is generated by moving averages which help traders identify trends in the securities.

For a downtrend, the price of the security crosses below the middle band, and the middle band acts as a resistance for the price, as seen in the image below.

When the price of the security crosses above the middle band, an uptrend is seen, for which the middle band acts as a support for the price of a security.

The middle band is used best to trail the price of the security for a profit target.

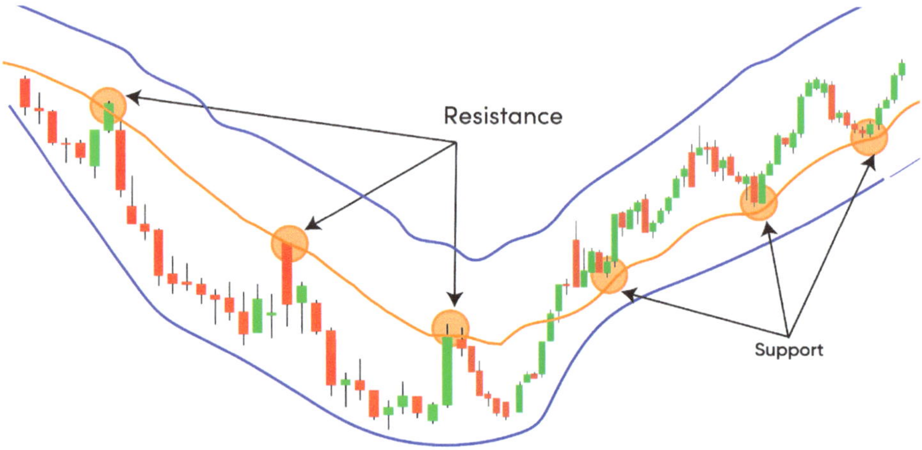

Fig. Trends With Bollinger Band

Range-bound markets with Bollinger Bands

The Range bound markets trade between a specific high and low over a specific period. Generally, narrow range Bollinger Bands indicator is preferred over widened bands in range-bound markets to spot high and low prices of a security.

When the price of a security is near to the lower band an entry to a new position can be placed or a short position can be squared off and vice versa.

Time frame to setup Bollinger Bands

As a trader, Bollinger Bands can be set to any time frame based on trading strategies.

For intraday setups, a lower time frame like 5 minutes or 15 minutes is preferred. For swing trades or position trades, the daily or weekly time frame is preferred for better entry/exit signals

5) MACD Indicator

MACD, an acronym for moving average convergence divergence, is a momentum-based trend-following indicator. This indicator consists of a MACD line, signal line and histogram which are based on the moving average of securities price.

Where,

- The MACD line and the signal line indicate entry and exit opportunities in the price of a security.
- The histogram represented over the zero line indicates bullish and bearish momentum present in the security.

As the moving averages diverge and converge, the MACD indicator oscillates, generating buy and sell signals in security.

The indicator prefers an exponential moving average (EMA) rather than a simple moving average (SMA) as a base to plot because EMA gives more weightage to the recent closing price of a security.

Formula to calculate MACD indicator

The MACD indicator uses a default value of 26 EMA, 12 EMA and 9 EMA, and it is calculated as explained below.

- MACD line: short-term EMA – long-term EMA.
- i.e. 12 EMA – 26 EMA.
- Signal line: 9-period EMA
- Histogram: It is a difference between the MACD line and the Signal line that oscillates above and below the zero line.

What does histogram signify?

- The histogram becomes positive when the MACD line is above the signal line.
- The histogram becomes negative when the MACD line is below the signal line.
- The histogram will become zero at the point MACD and signal line crossover.
- The histogram becomes larger or shorter when the MACD line and signal line widen or converge, respectively.

Trading strategies with MACD indicator

The MACD indicator helps traders develop strategies to find entry and exit opportunities with potential views and well-defined risk-to-reward ratios. Following are the different strategies you can employ using the MACD indicator.

Crossover strategy

The MACD line and the signal line crossover of the indicator signals entry and exit opportunities in a price of security.

When the MACD line crosses above the signal line, it indicates a potential uptrend, and one can enter a long position in the security to capture upward movement and place a stoploss a few points below the entry.

Also, one can book the profits in a long position when the MACD line crosses below the signal line.

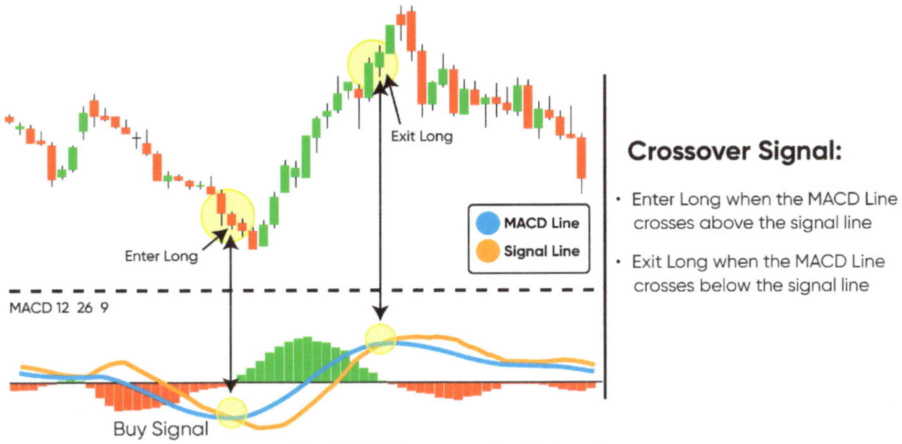

Fig. MSCD Crossover for Uptrend

When the MACD line crosses below the signal line of the indicator, it indicates potential downtrend and one can enter a short position in the price of security to capture downward movement and place a stoploss a few points above the entry. Also, one can book the profits in a short position when the MACD line crosses above the signal line.

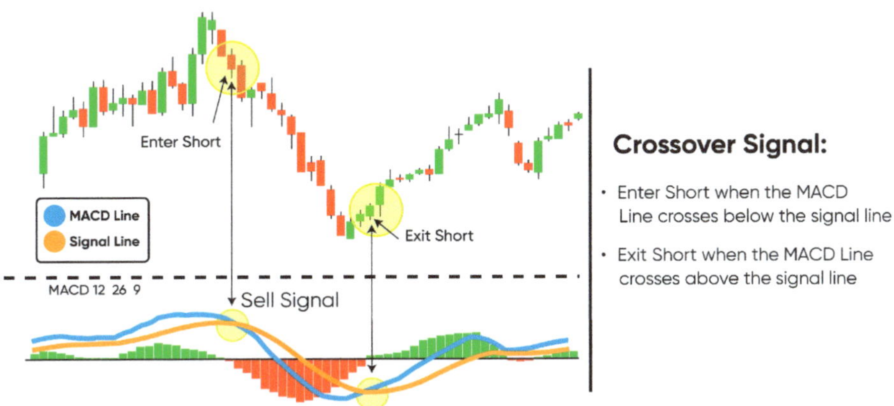

Fig. MSCD Crossover for Downtrend

Divergence in MACD

MACD divergence occurs when the price of a security is trading in opposite direction to the change in momentum of a MACD indicator. There are two types of MACD Divergence: Bullish Divergence & Bearish Divergence

Bullish Divergence

A bullish divergence is formed when the price of a security makes a lower low, but the MACD indicator is diverging by higher lows. This shows that bullish momentum in the security can be expected and one can take longs in the market with strict stop loss, a few points below the entry.

As a confirmation, entry can be placed after the MACD line crosses above the signal line of the indicator.

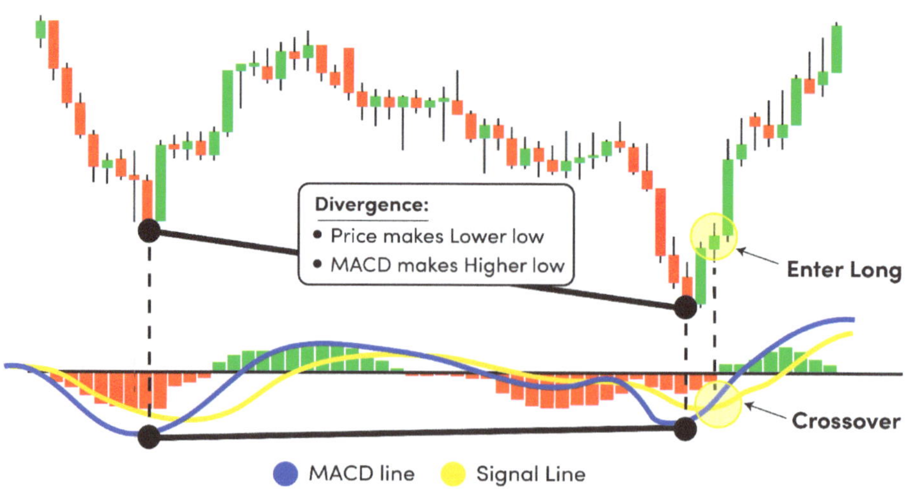

Fig. MSCD Indicating Bullish Divergence

Bearish Divergence

A bearish divergence is formed when the price of security records a higher high but the MACD indicator forms lower highs. Here, the weaker momentum formed in the MACD signals to take a short position or exit the long position. For short positions, one can place Strict Stop loss, a few points above the entry.

It is advised to take a confirmed trade once the MACD line crosses below the signal line of the indicator.

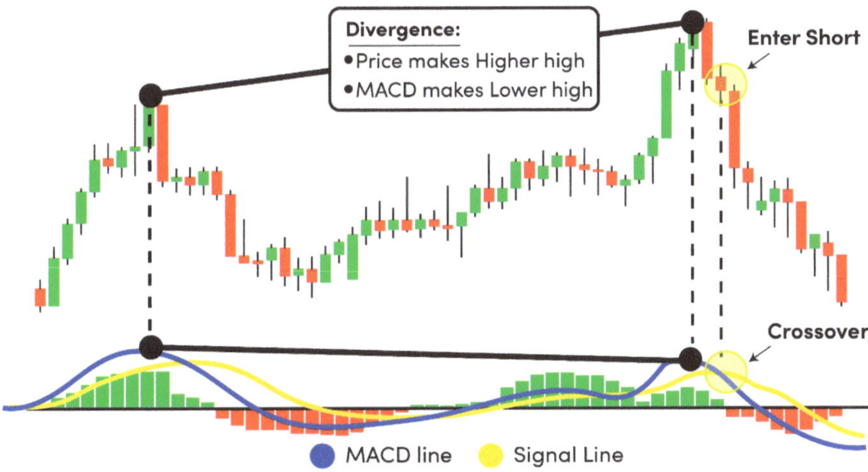

Fig. MSCD Indicating Bearish Divergence

In this chapter, we covered five of the most important technical indicators. A few other popular indicators that are also commonly used are Supertrend, VWAP, Ichimoku cloud, On-Balance volume, CCI, etc. It is advised to the traders to backtest all these indicators to understand their accuracy and implementation before using them directly in the live market.

TRADING PSYCHOLOGY & RISK MANAGEMENT

In the last chapter of this book, let us discuss the most important aspect of trading, which is way more important than any other technical aspects like charts, indicators, etc, that we have discussed so far. This is known as Trading Psychology. If you want to become a successful trader, you need to have a strong trading psychology, which includes the ability to control your emotions during trades, think fast and be disciplined.

If we look into why Trading psychology is so important, it is because trading psychology explains why some traders are more profitable than others, though they all may have an equal skill set. It also explains the ability of the trader to make rational decisions, avoid panicking, and stick to their informed resolutions in times of crisis.

Before we discuss the key points to know in trading psychology, let us first discuss three of the most prominent blunders committed by newbie traders that they should avoid:

1. Fear of Missing Out (FOMO) leading to Quick Positioning

   A prevalent misstep among inexperienced traders is impulsively taking positions so that they do not miss out on the big moves. However, this practice frequently results in significant losses.

When you're looking into buying a stock at Rs 100, and within a minute, it goes to Rs 105, the general fear of missing out on the opportunity comes to the mind of every trader. Though traders should act quickly, it should be based on Rational decision and not out of FOMO. The same share can come down to Rs 90 within minutes and lead you to losses if you haven't analysed it properly. The market will always give opportunities, and one should not trade based on FOMO.

2. Misjudging Risk and Reward

Many novice traders are willing to accept a loss of 5,000 but hastily lock in profits as soon as they see 1,000 on their screens. They might be comfortable with sticking to the trade till the Stop Loss (SL) hits but lack the patience to hold a trade until it reaches the target price.

This skewed risk-to-reward ratio is not permissible to sustainable profitability. To increase the odds of success, always aim for a risk-to-reward ratio of at least 1:1 or, or higher.

POWER OF 1:2 RISK:REWARD

Win Rate= 40%	
Trades	P&L
6x Losses	-6%
4x Wins	+8%
Total	+2%

Win Rate= 50%	
Trades	P&L
5x Losses	-5%
5x Wins	+10%
Total	+5%

Win Rate= 60%	
Trades	P&L
4x Losses	-4%
6x Wins	+12%
Total	+8%

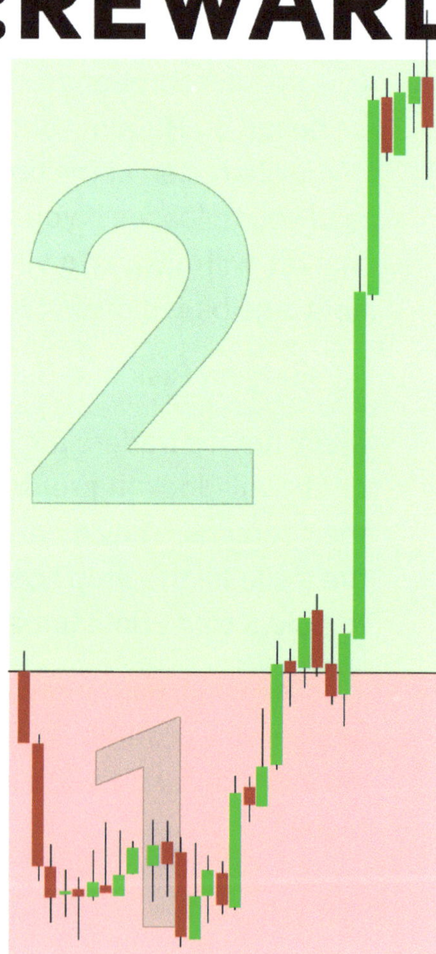

3. Wrong Position Sizing

Even traders with very little experience often engage in trades involving huge quantities. If a trade moves 10 points in their favour, they make a big profit, but if it goes against them by 10 points, they also incur a hefty loss. After this single unsuccessful trade, the dangerous "revenge psychology" may kick in, leading beginners to overtrade and suffer even greater losses.

When learning to trade, it's essential to anticipate the possibility of a trade going wrong and calculate potential losses if the Stop Loss is triggered. Always consider how much you are comfortable losing before entering any trade. Trading with smaller quantities can help mitigate these risks.

Now, let us discuss a few of the most important trading psychological points to know as a trader that would help you improve your trades

1. Avoid Over-Analysis Paralysis

   Many traders face the dilemma of Over-Analysis Paralysis while trading. They tend to over-analyze and over-research the trades before executing them. Many times, this leads to trade being missed. Too much information sometimes overcomplicates trading. As there are hundreds of indicators and chart patterns available for traders, using all of them at the same time may lead to uncertainty in decision-making. A trader should stick to simple analysis and not over-complicate the trade.

2. Not maximizing the trade vs Holding Too Long

   Not maximising your trade and holding on to a trade for too long are two sides of the same coin. As discussed earlier, as a trading mistake, we tend to book our profits too quickly and not maximise the potential. If your goal for trading is to make maximum profits, there is no reason to book just because you are making some money.

Nonetheless, one should not hold on to a trade for too long even if the market is showing a change in momentum. Do not always have a viewpoint of what if I book too early if the market is showing signs of reversals. Remember that Profit in hand is better than profit in books, and one should try to go home with at least some profits by the end of the day if the trade was in their favour.

3. Understand the Randomness of the Market

   An important point to believe and accept for all traders is that the markets are random to a large extent. Many times, the market will do such random things that cannot be explained by either fundamentals or technicals and both of these work only to an extent. As long as you, as a trader, are in sync with the randomness in the market, try to maximise the possibility.

4. Accept when you are wrong

   One of the most difficult art for humans is to accept when one is wrong. While trading, you are your own worst enemy if you don't accept when you're wrong, as this might lead you to wipe out a big chunk of your capital if you acted otherwise. Instead, accept when you're wrong, and it will help you avoid the chain of other wrong trades.

5. Do not revenge against the market

   Understand the fact that the market is too big for you to take revenge. Never have the mentality to take revenge against the market. We need to remember that we, as individual traders, are a part of the market, and we cannot trade without the market. Moreover, it would not make any difference to the market, if a small trader like you or me were there in the market or not.

Trading psychology is the most important aspect of trading that every trader needs to learn. In this book, you have learned about the various technical charts, patterns and indicators. However, you need to learn a sound trading psychology in order to implement what you have learned, and it will require time and experience from your side.

Mastering Candlestick Strength

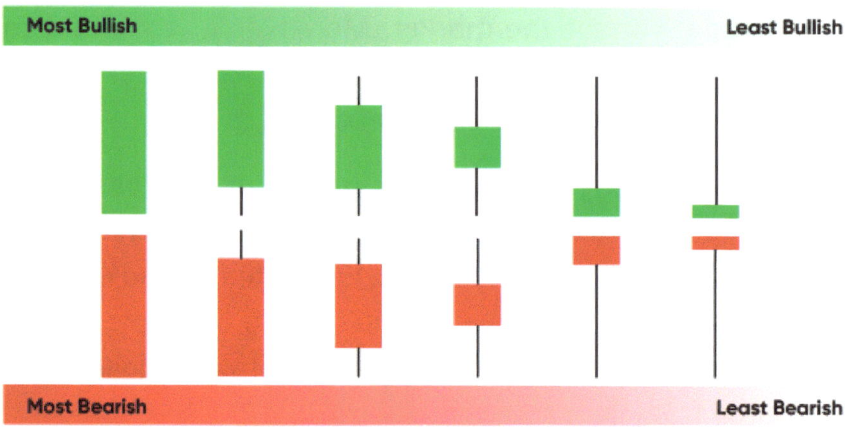

4 DIFFERENT TYPES OF TRADING STRATEGIES

Parameters	Scalping	Day Trading	Swing Trading	Position Trading
Trading Time Frame	Short term	Same day	Medium Term	Long Term
Trading Signals	Many Signals Daily	Few Signals Daily	Few Signals Weekly	Few Signals Monthly
Typical Holding Time	Minutes	Hours	Days or Weeks	Months or years
Chart Interval Analysis	1 Min 3 Min 5 Min	5 Min, 15 Min, 30 Min	1 Hr, 4 Hr, 1 Day	Days, Weeks, Months
Trade Monitoring	Very active	Active	Moderately Active	Rarely Active

Candlestick Patterns Cheatsheet

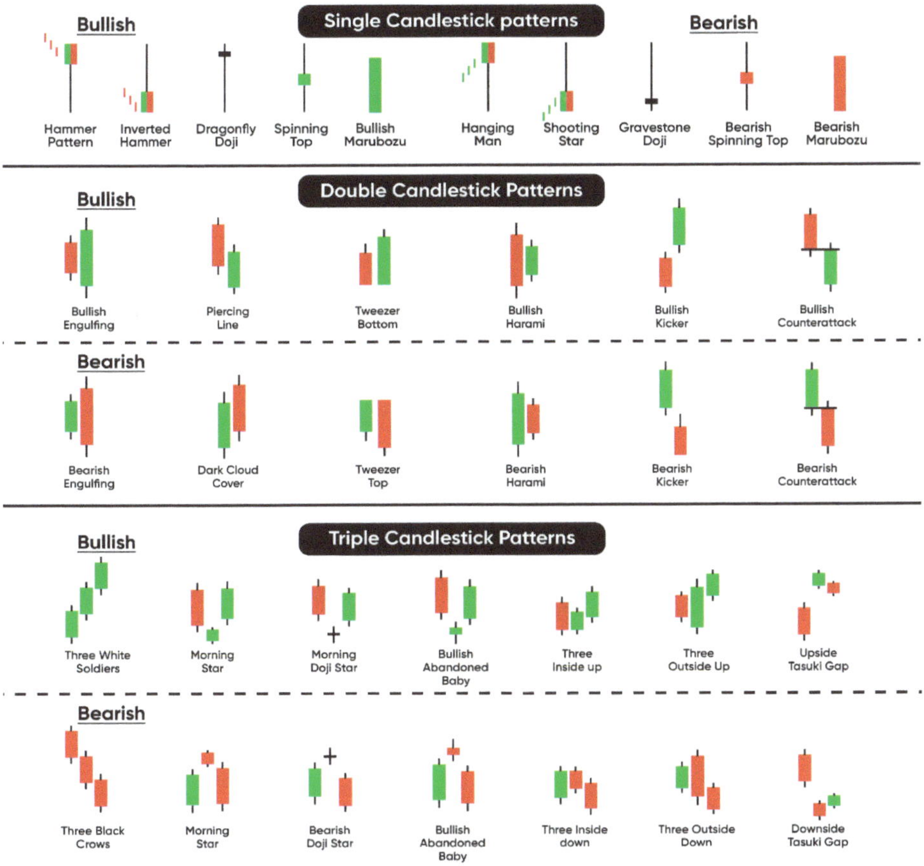

Fig. Candlestick Cheat Sheet

(Image Credits: joinfingrad.com)

Technical Indicators Cheatsheet

Relative Strenght Index

Indicates the overbought and oversold zones.

Fibonacci Retracement

Identifies S&R level using retracement levels from fibonacci sequence.

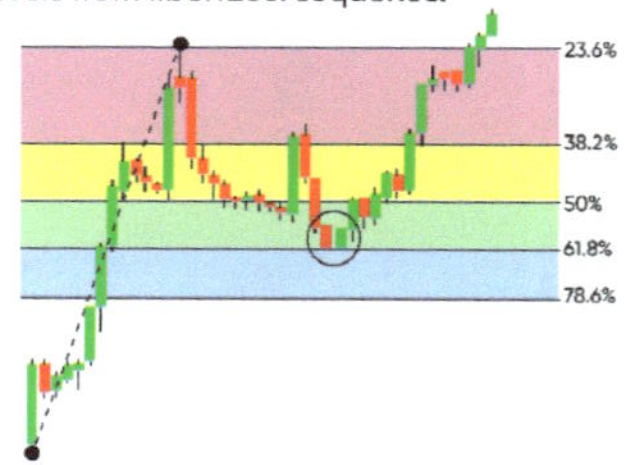

Price Volume Trend

Indicates the money flowing in and out of the security.

Average True Range

Indicates market volatility by measuring the average range between high & low price.

Fig. Leading Indicators

MACD Indicator

Measures the relationship between two moving averages of a security to identify potential trend reversal or strenghts.

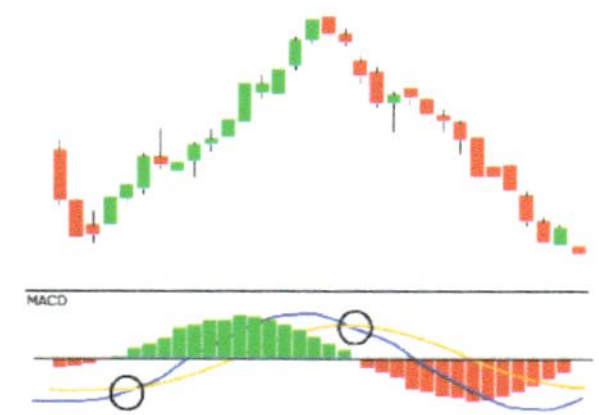

Moving Averages

Signals smoothed price trends that helps in spotting market trends, reversals, and prevailing sentiment over a set period.

Bollinger Bands

Indicates price volatility and potential reversal points by measuring the standard deviation of a securities price around a moving average.

Parabolic SAR

Helps in identifying the direction of the trend and potential entry or exit points in the market.

Fig. Lagging Indicators

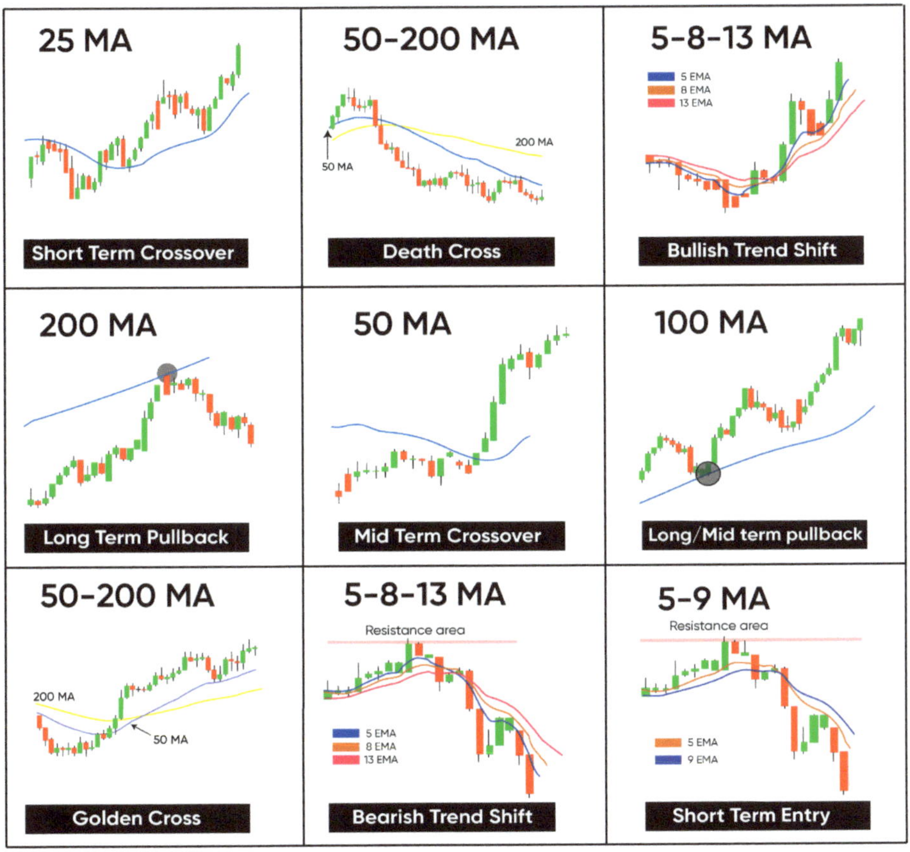

Fig. Moving Averages Cheat sheet

Chart Patterns Cheatsheet

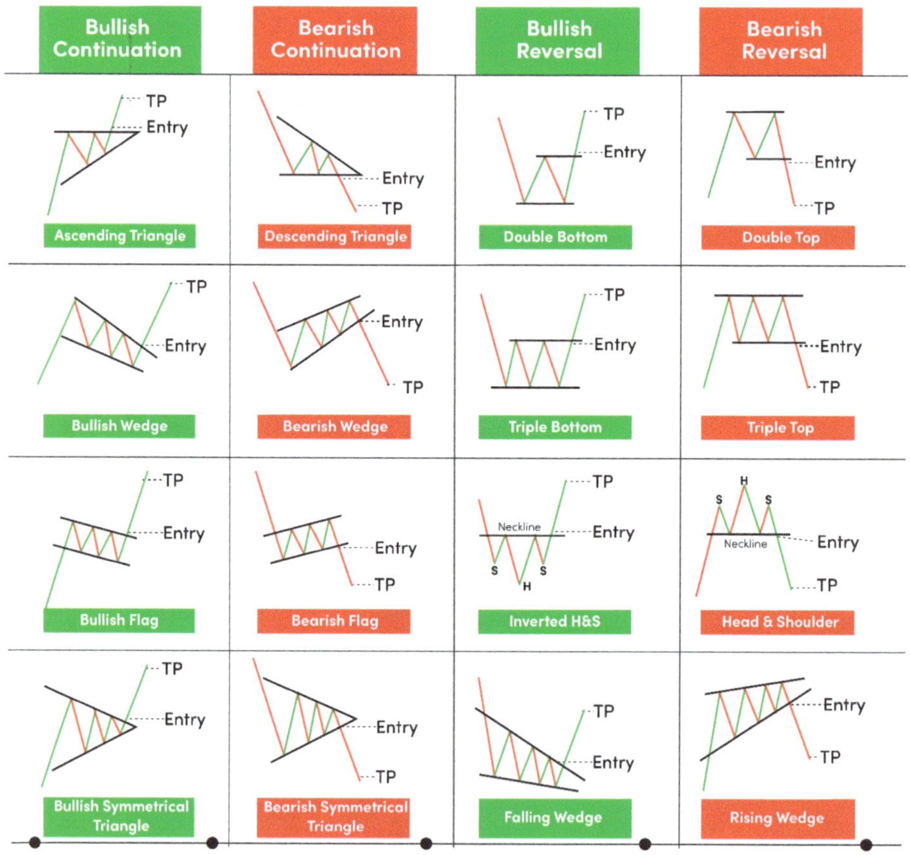

(Image Credits: joinfingrad.com)

www.ingramcontent.com/pod-product-compliance
Lightning Source LLC
LaVergne TN
LVHW051134210926
848482LV00006B/306

9798893226997